Permission to be f*cking Happy

Sarah Miller

Permission to be f*cking Happy
ISBN: 978-1-7396178-0-6

First published in Great Britain
in 2022 through Amazon self-publishing
service Kindle Direct Publishing

Disclaimer: real names/places
have been changed to protect the identities.

Produced by Miss Digital Media

‘What you seek is seeking you’

~ Rumi

Contents

Dedication 7
Author Bio 9
1 The beginning of self-abandonment 11
2 You can't fake happiness 15
3 What's a tanorexic got to do with it? 23
4 When the green juices and spiritual healers just aren't quite hitting the mark 31
5 Happiness is like floating in the sea 41
6 Let's start growing something beautiful together 51
7 Who the f*ck are you? 57
8 Every choice I make makes me 73
9 You but mark 2 85
10 Accept it, change it or bloody well leave it! 101

11 Create some space to flourish 109
12 It's all about energy flow bro 115
13 How to work your earth wire 133
14 It's perfectly normal to howl at the moon 139
15 It's time to quit the shadow boxing 147
16 I couldn't be fake about anything; my facial expressions would give me away 155
17 The myth of the miracle pill 165
18 Stay away from bad vibes 171
19 Finding faith (whether you choose to believe in a God or not) 181
20 It's alright for her 205
21 Style your Best F*cking Life 215
22 Permission to be f*cking happy 221
Acknowledgements 225
Contact 228

Dedication

This book is dedicated to my amazing, inspiring, slightly crazy auntie, Judy. Your death gave me the permission to be happy, and I am living my life to the fullest, to make up for the life that you no longer get to live.

It is also dedicated to my two beautiful daughters. Firstly, I apologise for the swearing, but like I always say, there is a time and a place. You drive me to be the best I can be so that I can lead by example. You are my most precious gifts, and you will never know how deep the love goes. Thank you for being my most wonderful creations and the anchor that has kept me safe in the hardest of times.

Author bio

Sarah Miller is a forty-something, highly sensitive mum living in Surrey, UK, with her two girls and her cat. She is a retired marketeer, qualified personal stylist and biophilic interior designer, and self-diagnosed tanorexic. She now works as a lifestylist and writer, helping mid-life women to find happiness again by allowing them to re-gain their sense of self, reinforce their values and find their life vision.

1

The beginning of self-abandonment

For some reason, so many of us are led to believe that we are not worthy of care or that life should be hard, and if it isn't, we aren't doing it right. That we should work ourselves into the ground, hating our day-to-day lifestyle and that martyrdom over who is the most exhausted is to be hailed. This starts in the traditional workplace and then often spills over into parenting. The bickering over who most deserves a rest begins! Happiness is effectively a luxury that we can't afford. This thought process has often been instilled into us through our childhood experiences.

As a coping mechanism for the overwhelming speed that the hamster wheel of life can get up to in these "responsibility years", we neglect our SELVES (I write it in caps to really highlight how we have forgotten about our SELVES!). Our SELF is so important and so valid; when we speak about our SELVES, we refer to mySELF, but which of you are truly giving a shit about your SELF or believing that to do that is being selfish?

When did you last even have time to acknowledge that you are anything more than an overworked mother f*cker? You are going through the motions of life without having the energy or the foresight that this is it?! This is your one and only life and your shot at the title. This is where your happiness comes from, and it is the journey to be revered. The one and only chance you have to play the game. Whilst you are distracted with your attention on the plates up in the air precariously spinning, you forget that there is a life to be lived. Not just 'coped with' or, in cases like mine, 'endured.' It is there to be lived in all of its f*cking amazing glory (i.e. your dream life but with some seriously shiny bells on) because what's the point otherwise?!

It is my mission to prove to you that none of this is true and that we are all, in fact, worthy of happiness, and it is only by embracing this that we can embody our true selves. I have learnt that actually choosing happiness (although that seems like a highly risky plan in some instances, as it was in mine) is, in fact, the path with the least resistance and thus the answer to your prayers.

Through this book, I want to share my journey and the painful truths that I learned along the way, including the far-reaching effects of self-abandonment. I provide you with the tools that I have used to take a risk on happiness to empower you to do the same so that you can be happy too and, with that, improve our collective lifestyle, health and those of our children and the generations to come.

We are the trailblazers, the leaders, the agents of change and the ones who may no longer be like a shiny penny but we have earnt the interest of experience and can use this to model a world where true happiness is the only goal. As we work together and make these changes, the universe will conspire to bring about what we wish were true to make it so.

I will give you permission to be happy and not just a little bit happy; I hereby give you permission to be f*cking happy.

2

You can't fake happiness

In this crazy life that we lead where we can literally have it all (and at the drop of a hat), overwhelm is by far the overriding setting and with that come its partners in crime; anxiety, worry and more worry. I can't even begin to convey the levels of overwhelm, anxiety and worry that I have experienced on my parent journey. Let alone as a single parent with no backstop.

Absolutely nothing prepared me for this, and it turns out that there is not much that can rob you of more joy than these three fuckers. And worry creates more worries that then create more worries, and then more and more and more (you see where I'm going). And then something happens to substantiate that worry and reinforces that you were so right to have worried. Thank goodness you spent all of that time worrying in preparation for this event which proved you right!

At least you were mentally prepared for it, right? Self-fulfilling prophecy, perhaps? Have you ever been on that rocking horse of worry that takes you nowhere but steals your light, your life and your health? Worry breeds worry; we pass it onto our children like a disease, a pointless waste of time but something that our minds love to get their claws into. Overwhelm, anxiety and worry cause stress in our bodies and minds and then we begin to unravel.

As a mother to two beautiful little girls, I allowed the strain of all of these bastards to rob me of the joy of the most precious years of my children's lives. It was compounded by the fact that I was in an unhappy marriage and not living the life that I really wanted for myself. But at the time, I didn't have the headspace to even recognise that.

Or so I thought. Looking back, this worry was probably just an escape route to allow me not to face up to the actual truths of my life. I was living day by toxic day, getting through and pretending to all those around me that everything was just fine and that I was happy. I mean, I was a pro; I was so good at it. And admittedly, my life looked beautiful because I had created it that way. I have an innate ability to put on a brave face and to make everything look in perfect order from the outside when inside, I was an absolute broken mess.

Sometimes I would smile through the pain and hope that someone would see through the pretence and call me out on it. They would look deep into my eyes and say, 'you're not okay, are you?' It never happened. Turns out that I was waaaaaaay too good at the pretence of being happy. Even I believed I should be happy with my lot, but I was just such an ungrateful bitch. I didn't appreciate everything that I had, and that's why I was so miserable. And then I hated myself just a little more, which ate away at me.

Who wouldn't be happy with a picture-perfect barn conversion in beautiful countryside as their home? The two luxury cars on the driveway, exotic holidays and meals out? I was a member of the local country club, had a personal trainer, played tennis and entertained friends and family. Add a good-looking husband and two beautiful daughters that I got to spend all my time with - no work for me. And to cap it all off, the perfect black Labrador who was everybody's friend and entirely useless at being a gun dog.

It was then that I learnt the first of my harsh life lessons, and that was that you can 'pretend' everything is fine. However, our naughty SELVES actually notice what's going on and when you aren't living 'your truth.' The civil war inside your subconscious will show up in unexpected ways like chronic illnesses that can literally stop you in your tracks. My health gave me away in the end, and I was so cross with it for failing me! It made me address the problems in my life. But I know that it was a blessing. It just felt like a curse because I really didn't have time for it as I was too busy holding my life together by a thread.

Maybe you know how that feels? The random aches and pains keep appearing, your back and head hurt, chronic illnesses are kicking in, and the doctors can't explain them. You are beginning to wonder what the point is? Why is everything so hard? You question why you feel so unfulfilled? What's the meaning of life? Crikey!! It's a frightening place to be. I thought I was dying, but it turns out I was just falling apart (what a relief)!

If you aren't living in alignment with your value systems, you start to break like a home that wasn't built with the correct infrastructure for its environment. You are soon washed away when a wave crashes over you, derailing the system that you have put in place to convey happiness but has no roots in your own desires. It turns out that you can't fake happiness. Funnily enough, it defeats the object and is called 'toxic positivity' – who knew! More on that later.

You literally can't cheat the system. You are too clever. You are made to live by your beliefs, and when you have bent so far in the wrong direction, you break. Yes, you need to be adaptable to change and compromise, and flexibility and open-mindedness are key. But when you live out of alignment with your values, you break your mind, soul, and nervous system, and then your health plummets. You then default to self-neglect and worry - because what else is there to root you back down? The alternative is to face up to where you are and make conscious changes to your life before it's too late. That's beyond scary! I mean, worry is one thing but facing up to your current reality is another. I don't know about you, but when I hit 39, things were so bad that I had to rip the plaster off, and I tell you what…it f*cking hurt!! Blowing up the ship is an understatement, but change is not possible without making a bit of a mess. In my case, I was left with some smouldering ashes that seemed to be permanently under a rainstorm, but it was a new beginning, and nothing lasts forever.

Change is always good.

How frivolous that sounds but oh so essential. You literally can't afford to be unhappy these days; you don't have the time, and what is the point of wasting this one precious life? Once the plates come crashing down and you are left crying over the spilt milk on the kitchen floor, it is so important to rise again. Even with so much going on, it's vital that your infrastructure is grounded in self and your values are intact this time.

Your abandonment makes you harder, uglier, unkinder and less forgiving. The person that gets it in the neck first is also yourself! You become the mean girl that you've always despised. You rip yourself to pieces; god, I'm so wrinkly…when did I get so flabby? Why haven't I done any exercise? Why am I so lazy? Why can't I be more like her (insert name of your nemesis)? What's all that skin down there for? Where did that hair come from? Why is it on my nipples? OMFG, what is happening to me? Are those varicose veins? Have I got piles? Is that a turkey neck? Is this it? What have I got to offer now I'm old and worn? When did this happen? What's the point? Fuuuuuuuuccckkkkkkkkkkkk!!!

Once you have destroyed yourself with negativity and self-scrutiny, you then turn to your partner (if you have one). Then you drag them down with you as you wrap your legs around them and use them as your life support, sapping their energy as you vent your frustrations. Then the poor kids get the curse of the unhappy mummy. You are snappy and tired, your energy levels are low, and you have very little to give. You can only love your children unconditionally when they are in bed asleep. The tears are never very far away, and are they tears of sadness or frustration or mixed together? Life becomes hard, overwhelming and a drag. The sunshine seems to be behind the clouds more than it is out. You watch your children's happy faces and wish that you didn't feel the way you do and could just relax into the world they live in before the cares became too much and all innocence was lost. You desperately want to be yourself again and feel safe with being that. It's called being self-assured… and as far as I know, it is the only route to happiness and is inexplicably linked to the state of your health.

3

What's a tanorexic got to do with it?

So, who am I, and why am I writing this book? Sometimes I ask myself the same question when I'm due at a school assembly, the life admin is piling up, and I'm not sure if there is any food in the fridge for dinner!

My name is Sarah (you probably got that from the cover), and I am a highly sensitive, mid-life mum of two little girls (who aren't so little anymore). I am somewhere between a librarian and a hedonist (depends on which energy I am feeding). I crave sunshine (officially a tanorexic, and I'm so pleased that this is a recognised condition that I can claim). I also love the water (termed as a hydrophile – who knew!). I'm pretty obsessed with the concept of positive luxury.

I want to spend the rest of my life travelling worldwide, visiting barefoot luxury retreats with spas. Either nude or in a bikini/robe - just for decency at the breakfast table. I go a bit squishy inside for hermit crabs, socks and nature (in particular plants, beaches, mountains and any form of water). Also, grey t-shirts (but I don't like grey skies) and beautiful aesthetics…oh and my two little girls and all my nieces and nephews except for one (just kidding).

I blew the ship on my life and left my marriage when I was on the brink of turning 40, and my little girls were 1 and 4. I left because I was seriously unhappy and didn't want my children to think that mum being seriously unhappy and all the perks that came with that were normal. Leaving my marriage left me homeless, penniless and pretty broken mentally. Who wants a washed-up 40-year-old mum who seems to have lost her spark and the wrinkles have set in big-time? I think hopeless is the word. I had zero concept of how hard life would be after making such a dramatic change. The domino effect of that decision was huge. It changed the trajectory of my life. I didn't just walk away from marriage; I walked away from the entire infrastructure and safety of my life. They suggest that life begins when we get out of our comfort zone. I did an out of the frying pan into the fire covered in flammables. Nothing would ever be the same again, and the monumental rebuild ahead of me seemed impossible.

Losing the entire infrastructure of my life and taking responsibility for the ashes that were left has been beyond hard (particularly as an empath). I have had several dark nights of the soul (I just assumed one only had one, but it appears not in my case). These times dragged me to my lowest ebb; they were effectively hell on earth. There were times when I questioned whether I had the strength to continue this life journey. I wanted to be like Sleeping Beauty, go to sleep for a very long time and wake up to the kiss of my one true love (ideally a Prince but not Andrew) saving me from my life. It didn't happen; it doesn't happen. Kids stay away from Disney.

In the midst of this, I was also trying to rebuild my career to earn money to provide for my children and myself. I was claiming working tax credits, child tax credits and child benefits. You name it; I was claiming it as I was stuffed financially. My health was shot to pieces; at the same time, I was re-locating and re-housing myself and the kids to be nearer my family. Parenting was ongoing (err, just keeping them alive) while going through an acrimonious divorce - all whilst trying to retain some semblance of hope for the future. There was no time to breathe. My career was five years behind me. I had worked as an Account Director in a Promotional Marketing Agency in leafy Wimbledon Village. I had totally taken my eye off the ball when I had kids (I was a lady who lunches) other than retraining as an Interior Designer (which was always the dream). During that time, the whole marketing arena had changed whilst I'd been knee-deep in nappies with Social Media hitting our phones and me entirely clueless about this happening. Gawd, life sucks sometimes!

So, I worked as a freelance marketeer and copywriter. To start with, I really enjoyed it because my client was a luxury furniture company based in the South of Spain (and a friend of the family). I got to take business trips over there and still be kinda involved with interiors and all the feels that created for me. Plus, I grew up in the South of Spain, so I hugely welcomed any excuse to go back as I could also visit my dad. After that, I started taking on more entrepreneurial clients who did the kind of things that I wanted to do. I focussed on lifestyle, health, wellbeing and clean beauty because these were the things that I was super passionate about. I retrained in social media. I worked with some really cool clients, but I was still unfulfilled.

During my dark nights of the soul, I looked really

hard at myself and my situation. I turned to coaches and therapists for help dissecting where I was at and why I couldn't seem to find any fulfilment. I constantly worked on improving my health. I looked at my situation…a struggling single mum, and I just found it so hard to identify with it. Did I need to dress differently to be that person? Did I need to show up differently? I found it so absorbing, and because I love style and aesthetics so much, I trained in Personal Styling with the London College of Fashion as I thought that perhaps being a stylist would be my jam. But that wasn't it. I love style, but I class myself as a sophisticated hippie. I like looking nice, but I also don't like a lot of stuff…I like quality over quantity, and sustainability is really important to me, and the thought of being a personal stylist just felt wrong. I couldn't be that light-hearted; for me, style is about expressing exactly who you are, not about following any trends. I knew that I had so much more to give. I had discovered much more about the psychology behind self-image, which was a major factor in the person I wanted to be and how I identified with myself and the world around me.

Finding a sense of fulfilment and purpose in my life and setting an example to my little girls to follow their hearts and, most of all, believe in themselves is what drives me forward. The human spirit is pretty indomitable, and it is hard to quash it. We all need a challenge to rise, and the bigger the challenge, the higher we rise (quelle surprise)! FML. My experiences meant that I needed to do more than just get through the rest of my life. I hadn't gone so low to live a mediocre life stuck on the hamster wheel and living hand to mouth; there must be more to it. I had to work on getting myself off the ground and put back together again, but this time in alignment, with all of my values intact and with a strong sense of self-belief. The one BIG BIG lesson I have learnt is that no one, and I mean no one, can save you but yourself. You are in charge of your life. You get to choose how it plays out.

You get to style a life that suits you, and no one can tell you otherwise. Because if you constantly listen to others like I did and don't start trusting yourself and your desires, you are royally f*cked. I'm just kidding. It's not a great place to be, but don't panic because the solution lies in the problem, and once you can see that, it's basically like being enlightened!! Yay! Hello Buddha, I made it! I took a few wrong turns, but that's part of the game, isn't it?

Once I had grasped this concept, I was like a dog with a bone; I started to turn my life around. Things made so much more sense, I was more fulfilled, and I became evangelical about my findings! What seems like a lifetime later and never-ending personal growth (call me Bridget Jones), I am here writing this book. I want to share my experiences and the challenges that I have overcome to find the thing that has eluded me for so long - HAPPINESS. Happiness will not mean that you are singing from the rooftops every day, as life doesn't work that way. But I can guarantee that once you have your infrastructure that allows happiness and, subsequently, health to thrive, you know that its potential is always there, and that is the opposite of hopelessness. I've been there, and it sucks. So this book is here, so you don't have to go to that sucky place. If you are currently residing there, let me reach out my hand and pull you back above the water, put my arms around you and tell you that you will be okay in all your broken and imperfect beauty and I will help you. I want you to be able to find that too.

4

When the green juices and spiritual healers just aren't quite hitting the mark

Plastering over the cracks is often how we deal with challenges when our life is going at speed. It's not often that it's simple enough to make a slight change of direction without causing any collateral damage. Change is hard, and the problem must first be ripped apart for any change to be successful. But we all know that those plasters lose their stickiness over time, and the blood and gore that it was covering goes mouldy and putrefied, and unless we take the plaster off and let the wound breathe, it won't heal.

I mean, I'm considering ending the book there because if we could all just sit and breathe and stop doing for a reasonable amount of time, we might get back to ourselves. But it's not as simple as that in this full-on life that we lead. I did try just sitting with myself and permitting myself to do nothing, but it's not in our nature to do that unless we have given ourselves over fully to the service of God. Although even your average monk still debates and has active propulsion forward. I've seen them in Tibet, wildly alive but calm and centred. We are not designed to stop growing. I found it depressing. More depressing. I had so much time to think, and thinking is something that I am excellent at, whether it is thinking myself over the edge of a cliff or simply into an early grave.

I don't know about you, but I tried everything in my pursuit of happiness. It started when I picked up a book at the airport on the way to visit my Dad. It was my first trip away alone without my kids, my divorce was going through, and I had an 11.5-hour flight to Canada to contend with, along with my thoughts (oh god, anything but my thoughts). I must admit that I'm not the greatest flyer anymore, but I love to travel, so that's annoying. To say that I was terrified of everything at that point was an understatement; my nervous system was on a high, high, red alert! Warning, warning, if you step onto this plane, it will surely crash (that was my thought process at the time).

Anyway, back to the book that I picked up at the airport; it was called Operation Happiness, and my hope from reading this book was that it would tell me how to be happy again! There would be a secret code within it that would turn my life around, and I would stop being so miserable. I had high expectations, and I devoured every word of it. BUT although I learnt so much, I was still miserable! I thought that I had strayed slightly off my path and just needed a little coaxing to get back on, and although my life had changed irrecoverably, I could just read a book, and everything would be okay again. Perhaps even a little more so because I thought that it would be that easy! I was just slightly deluded, but I think that was for the best.

From there, I tried everything that I could find to fix the mess I was in; CBT, NLP, EFT, RTT, breathwork and coaching. There were crystals, positive affirmations, clean eating, supplements, holidays, dating/not dating, reiki and cranial sacral therapy. Also massage, reflexology, personal growth books and workshops, pole dancing, boxing, pilates and even skipping. Then onto yoga, meditation, drinking/not drinking, spirituality, calling a psychic, tarot readings, numerology, therapy, spending/not spending, being super focussed and then being relaxed. I had house plants and a personal trainer; walking, sunbathing, having my nails done, botox and taking CBD oil. Each morning I drank Kombucha, matcha tea and celery juice. I tried the life-changing magic of tidying, motivational podcasts, and oil pulling - you get my drift. I'm sure you have been there too and, like me, probably spent a fortune on all of these. In my case, it all perpetuated the cycle of worry about finances and the necessity to do more of these activities to calm me down! Crazy!

I remember a very early experience on my healing journey when I had cranial sacral therapy that my auntie recommended. The therapist asked me to remember a time when I was happy, and then we could programme that into my mind so that when I pressed the middle of my palm, those feelings would come flooding back. I loved the concept. I just couldn't remember a happy time or what happiness even felt like (I said that I had thought of something just to breeze over this awkward concept). It makes me cry to write that, to know that I did not know this feeling any longer. Happiness wasn't in my emotional toolkit. I didn't know how it felt.

My next profound experience was reiki with my wonderful friend's mum, who happened to be a reiki master. I don't know if the reiki did anything for me, I couldn't feel anything, but one thing she said stayed with me, "when you don't know where to turn, turn to your health." It has helped me hugely.

Yeah, it sounds f*cking boring. Initially, it is; but I

have been on a huge wellness journey since then. I have learned that health and wellness involve a lot of placeboes and for placebo to work, enjoyment has to be involved - but I'll get into that in more detail in a later chapter.

My coaching experience wasn't so great. I took on a high-end coach at vast expense, way beyond my means. She convinced me that I needed her and that without her, I was hopeless. I came away from that experience broken again. I wasn't ready for a high-end coach. I was a mess. I didn't know who I was. Again I looked for a quick fix and a way to reach for the stars and someone to springboard off of. She made me feel like a complete failure and a failure who was now in some serious debt again that I couldn't pay off. Man, that f*cking hole hurt so badly. I beat myself up about how foolish I had been. I had been manipulated again. The scenario was familiar to me, and I ended up broken and in debt again. What kind of idiot was I? Have you ever done that? Thought that you were doing the right thing, and then when it doesn't work out, you berate yourself for thinking that you could have thought that you could trust yourself to make the right decision? I undermined myself by letting her have the power over me.

I didn't have the strength to fight back. I had to suck it up. I lost a little bit more faith in mankind.

My psychic experience was a little more positive; 6 years ago, she told me that I would be a hugely successful writer (but I ignored that because it sounded boring!) and that I would know true happiness at 43. My 43rd birthday came and went, and so did my last semblance of hope as the candles fizzled out, and my children clapped.

You continue to try out all the "methods" that are out there to help you fix yourself and listen to all the spiritual healers, and not of them is hitting the mark because they ARE NOT MIRACLE WORKERS.

There is no one size fits all, and they do not deal with the fundamentals of your infrastructure, and that is your values system and your 'self' and how you align with everything in your life. Does that make sense? We are all entirely different but inherently the same, which is even truer for us highly sensitive souls. You FEEL things so deeply! You can't not. You must learn how to deal with this superpower and use it to your advantage (because there are huge advantages). Only you are the miracle worker, and I promise you that there are miracles to be had out there, but it begins and ends with you.

Now don't get me wrong; I'm not saying don't do these things; these are all amazing ways to support your lifestyle, help you grow, be the best version of yourself and enjoy life. I bloody love growth, but there's a lifetime journey involved in becoming, and I'll get on to hands-on healing treatments a bit later, but as a HSP, they rock. The thing is (and this was so true for me), sometimes we just don't know where we want to go and who we want to be along the way. This makes it virtually impossible to know how to get there and what activities/uses of energy (physically, mentally and financially) will support us in getting there. We are just plastering over the cracks repeatedly and spending a lot of money doing a shoddy job whilst the damp creeps back in.

Answer me this; have you ever really taken the time to step back from the hamster wheel of life and think about who you are and how you want the rest of your life to pan out since you hit mid-life?

I am lucky to have had a major mid-life crisis triggered by my divorce, and I am massively pro a mid-life crisis (although I think we should call it a mid-life awakening for positivity's sake), but f*ck that! It's a crisis! Because if you were so enlightened already, it would never have happened (IMO), but it is essential, and it is a massive positive as it gives you the self-awareness and desire to live a happy and fulfilled life. I do not wish that on you. However, my lovely reader, my wish for you is that this book will save you from having to reach the depths that I did.

It is pretty easy (as I have learnt) to blindly step onto a moving walkway that has taken you an awful long way from yourself and the life that you want to live. Unless you have the presence of mind to step off and take the time to look at where you are now and acknowledge that perhaps some elements of your life aren't serving you, nothing will change (or that you are lucky enough that a major challenge comes and knocks you off wrecking ball style). Do you get me? It's called course correcting, and some of you will need to do more course correcting than others (there are no prizes for who must do the least) because it takes strength to face up to where you are at and make a conscious change. And it's hard, it's f*cking hard, but it is entirely worth it. A moment's pain for the rest of your lifetime's gain. Are you ready to do it? I hope so because it's from here to eternity!

Being able to get your head above water for long enough to breathe, assess where you are and then make changes to your direction to live in alignment with your 'self' and your values is brave. It's not just brave, it's f*cking amazing, and it's the only way to be happy and live your truth truly. The downside is that it is bloody scary. There is no roadmap, there are no guarantees, and the only way forward is to find faith in yourself; I'm guessing that if you are reading this book, you have lost a bit of faith in yourself and the future.

But imagine a life where you knew who you were and what you wanted from life, and you literally just did what made you happy. With the happiness came self-assuredness, and with both of those pillars in place, your health just fell into line? Imagine doing nothing more than just trusting your intuition and leaning towards joy (I say that through gritted teeth as it feels like such an overused word), but it's so true. Why are we so obsessed with making life so f*cking hard? It doesn't need to be. It really doesn't. And the more you burn out doing shit that you hate and living a life out of alignment, the more you will need to invest in repairing your health, both physically and mentally. Please hear my battle cry!

So, let's stop that way of thinking and start thinking that maybe, just maybe, life is actually meant to be fun. I don't mean non-stop party fun but just really enjoyable without any massive catches; although everything in life is a catch 22 (and I'll talk more about that later), we choose which aspect of the catch 22 we see. Like the glass half full or half empty. We can think that life is hard and harsh and unfair or believe it is happy, fun, light and supportive. I have seen and experienced enough suffering to last me a lifetime, but I choose gratitude. The key to our happiness is inside us, but it is very easy to lose your keys if you're anything like me.

But I'm going to help you find that key again if you want me to because it's a pretty important one.

5

Happiness is like floating in the sea

On a recent trip to see my therapist (check me out), she asked me that question again that my cranial sacral therapist had asked years ago that had been baffling me for a long time; "tell me about a recent experience of feeling happy?"

Have you ever asked yourself that question? Can you tell me when you last felt happy? I hope you can, but I assure you that you are not alone if you can't. Just her asking me had me sobbing because I finally knew the answer after not being able to answer it for over six years, and it was such a relief. A relief to know that I wasn't completely broken and a relief that I could finally answer her question but with so much compassion for the fact that I hadn't been able to. I thought I was being stupid rather than simply being incredibly unhappy.

Happiness is like floating in the sea. It is totally related to ease and feeling supported. It is only through weighing yourself down with worries, troubles, frustrations, overwhelm, and purposelessness that you keep yourself somewhere under the water's surface, occasionally breaking through to breathe. I had always been looking for exact moments in time when I felt particularly happy. But I could never get them to solidify. Finally, I had it cracked.

When you remove all of the weights that hold you down, you give yourself the freedom to revert to your natural state and pop straight back up above the water, where you can breathe freely. Yes, there will be stormy seas, and sometimes it will be harder to breathe than others; but there will also be calm seas where you can just lay back and bask in the sunshine and wonder at the magnificence of nature in all its crazy glory. But it's not all plain sailing (wow, I apologise for the number of analogies and metaphors in this chapter); life can literally change like the weather (and with the weather), and this is when you need to have your anchor in place.

Your anchor ensures that even though you may get knocked around by the rough seas, high winds and driving rain, you are still in the same place once you come out the other side, just a slightly more bedraggled version. Once I faced my fears and pushed through them with a powerful intention and vision of where I wanted to get, I could course correct whatever challenges hit and buffeted me through the storm. I was able to shake off the water so much quicker than previously when I would be out of action for a long time, licking my wounds and blow drying my hair. It sounds easy, but it isn't, and it took a lot of trying and failing to find myself. And then, when I had found myself, I had to accept who I was (ouch) and then find faith in myself; so that when the storms hit, and the waves crashed, I didn't drown but learnt to dive straight into them (and we all know that the best way over is sometimes through - particularly when it comes to rough seas).

Happiness is a state of mind. It's not as simple as saying I was last happy when I took my girls to the beach, the sun shone, we saw friends, and it was fun, and life felt good because it didn't. I was scared shitless of my life, and although we were doing all the right things and it looked beautiful, my mind was shot to pieces. All I could think was that this moment of happiness was not going to last because I didn't trust myself/life to support me. It goes back to my infrastructure analogy; it takes a while to dig deep, strong foundations that will ground you in place and hold you safe. Those foundations are you. The core of you. The essence of who you are. They are the things that will keep you safe. They are all your happiness. And your faith. And your commitment to yourself. They are your sense of self. They are God.

To know myself, I had to lose myself. This was beyond hard. I was questioning everything that I knew about life - trying to do things that I 'should' be doing because society told me that that was what I needed to do. I'm sure you have been there before. The problem was that the 'need' and my values system didn't align. They didn't just not align, they were also at complete odds with each other, and for a highly sensitive soul, this equates to disaster! I was toeing the 'good girl' line and not doing what I wanted to do.

If you are really honest, do you relate to being a 'good girl'? I kept trying to rise by cheating my own system so that I could do what was expected of me and thus not become an outcast. N.B. Having strong values makes you very Marmite, as a recovering people pleaser (did anyone get out on bullshit lingo bingo with that?) I am much more used to just being a bland spread that you can't even taste, so I don't rock the boat.

Let me tell you this; rising out of alignment does

not work for any period for anyone. It eats away at your physical and mental health as you are effectively undermining yourself, and it doesn't like it, and it lets you know that!

When I rose in alignment were the magical times, they were the times when I followed my heart and trusted in myself and when that happened, the results were insane! Life colluded with me to achieve my goals. I had experienced "manifesting" before but buying my house after I divorced was a massive example of making the impossible possible by sheer willpower. But please note here that there was sheer willpower, intent, and absolute alignment with me. I had to trust my intuition when everyone around me doubted me. I knew it was mine, I wasn't trying to shoehorn something that didn't fit, and the desire was strong. I made it happen. I had no idea how to make it happen but just getting the ball rolling was the best I could do, and trusting that it would all come together.

This is not how I used to work. The old me would have thrown this out like the baby with the bathwater as a crazy idea that wasn't rational, logical or achievable. Fortunately, I didn't have time for any of that bullsh*t anymore.

When I put an offer in on my house, I had zero money (I was in tens of thousands of pounds worth of debt) and no income and not much income likely in the short term. Things didn't look good. But I knew that this house was my future and my stake in the ground to rise from. I called the estate agents and told them that I was a cash buyer, put in an offer under the asking price, and then went away and hoped for the best. I had nothing to lose.

The first random bit of universe collusion happened a few days later; I was at our local garden centre with my youngest daughter watching her on the soft play: Freezing and alone, thinking FML. There was a table of women chatting behind me, and I didn't take much notice until one of the women mentioned that she had had an offer on her house and that it was a cash buyer, and they didn't know who the woman was but that she was new to the area…NEWSFLASH It was me!!

OMG, I could barely stop myself from turning around and saying that it was me. She then told tell her friends about the offer put in that they hadn't accepted but also said the amount they would accept. I felt so bad sitting there listening in, I wanted to tell them who I was, but I recognised that it was a gift, a massive bloody gift. I just watched everything pan out, and I didn't really need to do anything but just enjoy it. The next coincidence was that the sellers' surname and my surname sounded incredibly similar, so whenever

I rang the Estate Agents for an update, they would literally tell me what was going on from the sellers' side. It got so bad that I would have to identify myself as 'the buyer' rather than give my name!

Whether any of this insider knowledge helped me secure the house, I'll never know but what I do know is that when I followed my heart and my happiness, self-belief kicked in. I became a powerhouse, and impossible things became possible because I felt supported.

Other people's opinions didn't bother me. I had my eye on the prize, and I wouldn't take it off for anyone because I wanted that house so badly for me and my girls. When you have that desire to achieve, and everything falls into alignment, the magic f*cking happens. You don't have to control it, manipulate it, or tread on people's toes. You are riding the wave.

True happiness is there for us all. The hardest part of finding it is believing that you deserve it and permitting yourself to have it so that you can assure your 'self' that everything is okay and thus become 'self-assured'!! GENIUS!! But do you believe that you deserve it? If you don't, let me tell you that you bloody do no matter how hopeless everything feels! If that doesn't get through to you, give me your address, and I'll come and slap you round the face with a wet fish until you believe me.

We all deserve it no matter what! Once you know that you are enough just as you are (thanks, Mark Darcy), life becomes easy, like a wind-up music box playing your favourite tune.

Yes, you will have to put some effort into the winding, but once you know what music you want to play, it takes very little effort to keep winding the key. When you are out of alignment and scatter gunning energy playing different music, you are a bit f*cked like I was. There were too many plasters holding together an outdated version of myself that was no longer serving me (and that's because she was tired and f*cking fed up with me asking her to do loads of sh*t that she hated, so she checked out). It was only when I found my jam that she started serving again! What a primadonna! Just joking, we all have a limit.

So, I will help you find the music you want to set your life to. And give you the motivation to keep winding the key so you can do the work with as much energy conservation as possible. The last thing you need is overwhelming and for your 'self' to check out.

Are you up for it? I want to hear a resounding yes!! And then you can literally dance along with a rueful smile on your face because you know what life is about now. The hamster wheel and spinning plates are a thing of the past, and you genuinely feel sorry for those who haven't mastered the art of living. Whoop whoop, anyone for Summertime by D.J. Jazzy Jeff and the Fresh Prince and a cocktail on the side?!

6

Let's start growing something beautiful together

Okay, so now we are getting to the super-duper exciting bit where I will give you the key to unlock your **authentic self** and everything she desires. Is anyone else feeling excited!? I am!

Once she's out, I will give you the methodology for implementing your infrastructure and creating your systems to nurture your **authentic self** because you can't have one without the other. Think of it like a seed that you wish to grow. You start by deciding what you would like to grow in your garden/home to make you happy. You plant the seed in nutrient rich soil for that specific plant/flower. You place it in the correct surroundings and give it the right amount of water, sun, care and chat that it needs to flourish. You pull up any weeds and remove any pests that might hinder its progress. You might also start it inside in the warmth in a smaller pot until it gets stronger and more robust. You will shelter it from extreme cold, heat, storms, acts of God etc. (TBH, that's my methodology for nurture in a nutshell, so if you take nothing more from this book than that, then you are onto a winner, but I suggest seeing it through to the end)! Once it blooms, you delight in it, and you continue to nurture and care for it. It becomes precious to you. You come to terms with the fact that nothing in nature lasts forever, and you enjoy the here and now.

When I started on my mission to change my life and be "happy and fulfilled", I had the methodology and desire for change and growth. But because I didn't know who I was or who I hoped to be, I found it so hard to apply. It was like watering an empty pot and putting it in the sun and hoping that something beautiful inside would grow without planting the seed. Funnily enough, when I nurtured an empty pot, all that seemed to flourish were the weeds. Because some of them looked pretty and had gone to the effort of growing, I didn't really know which ones to pull up. It was a confusing time. I spent a lot of energy but gained very little other than learning.

The same is true and vice versa. You can have the seed, but if you don't put it in the correct environment and give it the nurture and care it needs, it will never flourish. Just another unrealised dream that you never gave the chance to bloom. To truly flourish in life, we need to get to the root of "the who" we want to grow so that when it comes to nurturing, we do not waste energy watering in the wrong places, and you know which weeds to pull and pests to eradicate!!

But before we get into this in earnest, I want you to understand two key things: Intuition and desires, and I will touch upon each of these to get the most out of the exercise I want to do with you, but I will go into them later.

Firstly, intuition. Our intuition is effectively our soul guidance. It tells us what to do and communicates with us throughout our days. It is our gut feeling. It is unique to each of us. It is how we feel in the dark. It is not to be ignored because it undermines our 'self' when it is. It is our 'self'.

It is easy to lose our sense of self and thus our intuition through overwhelm, trauma and damage to our gut from internal and external stressors. We clench our tummies when we are stressed, which hinders our ability to digest and processed food and toxins put stress on our digestion to eliminate the crap that wasn't designed to be put into our bodies in the first place, masking the voice that guides us.

All this stress makes it hard to hear our intuition and 'self' speak anymore. Throw in a child or two and the other challenges of the 'responsibility years' of midlife, and it gets even harder. For the sake of this exercise, I want you to slow down, breathe and listen because your 'self' will speak to you, and she is pretty strong-minded and totally fed up with being ignored.

Let's move on to our desires (including jealousy, as that is just another form of desire). We are taught from a young age that to have desires is wrong. If you have some weird desires that you think aren't right, they probably aren't, but all other desires are your f*cking lifeblood!! It is pure spirit running through you! They make you come alive! They challenge you to grow! Without desires, no one would strive for anything; there would be no creations because no one would be arsed!

It's a bit like Covid Lockdown. If you are anything like me, I had a fair amount of time at home on my hands (albeit with two young children), and I could have focussed on creating anything, but I really didn't. I just chilled out, slowed down and enjoyed my kids, I had no desire for anything, but that and that was my desire at the time! When a desire hits you for something, it is your spirit saying to you:

"You are the chosen one.... let's go do this."

A desire isn't given to you that you can't possibly achieve because that is so messed up, right?! We don't have desires for any other reason. And jumping on the bandwagon of someone else's desires is also f*cked up because that ain't your path, girlfriend! Do not covet another's success or seemingly perfect life. Stay in your lane and absolutely don't compare yourself to anyone else. It's a total waste of time and energy because you can only compare eggs with eggs, and eggs only get fried, poached or scrambled. Comparison truly is another thief of joy. I tell you what, being divorced at 40 with young kids and zero money or career and the stress of life showing my age, I pretty much broke any semblance of hope that I had by comparing myself with the following:

1: My close friends who are super successful and live seemingly beautiful lives. I'm starting again from scratch and feel like a poor relation.

2: The mums at school who all knew each other and had a husband, and I felt like a complete outsider.

3: All the women making a huge success of their lives and overcoming massive challenges whilst doing what they love and playing it out on social media. Meanwhile, I was flailing around trying to emulate them and punishing myself for being such a failure.

4: All the younger women out there with no baggage,

beautiful bodies, their whole lives ahead of them and no wrinkles on their faces. I questioned why anyone would ever want to date me over them. What could I possibly offer?

It's been a long journey to discover that this is a painful and entirely pointless exercise to waste any time with. All you are doing is eating away at your sense of self rather than nourishing her, which will never be good. We are all wonderfully and crazily different and thus never treading on each other's toes. Just because someone has something you want, it doesn't mean that you can't have it too. You just get to have it on your own terms, not someone else's, and that's much more rewarding. Remember that life is a journey, our destination is mapped out by our **desires** (and they are constantly evolving), and our **intuition** tells us how to get there. No one else can do this for you. The joy of life is embracing this and rolling with the adventures these goons take you on. Once you know your 'self', you are ready to get onto the ride in earnest and trust that you know how to navigate the perils! A bit like Indiana Jones and the Temple of Doom, but hopefully with less doom and more fun!

7

Who the f*ck are you?

Possibly the hardest question that I have ever had to answer and a delightful recourse that I like to throw at people who are pissing me off in my mind. However, I tend to keep it to myself as a people pleaser. At the ripe old age of 40, I had to find out who I was and what I was made of to get my life back. It was a frightening look in the mirror, and it can be severely unpleasant, but it is the road to enlightenment so let's get messy N.B. no mirror is required unless you really want to do that, but a pen and paper are helpful as we are gonna write some shit down.

So who the f* ck are you, and what makes you tick? I want you to answer these questions in as much detail as possible, but I want you to go with what first pops into your head even if it feels completely nuts (although I am rapidly learning that the nuttier, the better). What

I am saying is don't hold back. If you are anything like me, you have held yourself back your entire life. It is time to really unleash her. Set her f*cking free. Let her have her say. She has been nagging away at you with frustration, moodiness, stress, backache and lack of fulfilment for a long time, and you have ignored her, so let's unleash the beast once and for all!! Once you release her, it is virtually impossible to cage her again, so be prepared. It's time for you to do the "inner" work! What a wanker I am!

EXERCISE ONE:

Write down who you see when you look in the mirror/ your mind. I'm not so bothered by the aspect of looking in the mirror because, ultimately, how you see yourself is all in your head.

(For example, when I first did this, my answers were: old, tired, puts on a good game face, growing out highlights, hair needs a trim, the face could do with a miracle, in relatively good shape for my age, wearing clothes that could do with being replaced etc.)

EXERCISE TWO:

Write down how you identify with yourself. What would you say if someone asked you to describe yourself to another person?

(For example, when I first did this, my answers were: struggling single mum, no career, totally lost, health isn't great, suffering from bouts of depression etc.)

Now I want you to put aside everything that you learnt from exercises one and two and just imagine that everything in your life dropped away and it was just you and endless possibility (which means no limitations at all!). Then who would you be? What does the voice inside you say? Let's give it a chance to answer you in detail by guiding it with some questions. But please, please, please, don't let reality kick in; this is like answering the question, 'if I won £20 billion on the lottery, what would I do with it?' It is also very much about not overthinking the answers. It's not a trick either, and your answers are just that…your answers. It doesn't matter if you think they are crazy or just saying that because you must have heard it somewhere. That's the whole point.

Your subconscious brain, which does 95% of the work, knows all the answers (that's what the spiritual gurus mean when they say it is all inside of you), but society has taught us to only listen to the conscious brain, which only accounts for 5% of all the brain capacity. The subconscious brain is responsible for us breathing. You don't have to think about breathing to remember to do it (although breathing is something that we neglect in our hurried lives and need to go back to!). You trust that it just happens; otherwise, you would be pretty f*cked. We want to overrule the thinking brain, which can think us into an early grave. We wanna chat with the guru who lives behind that gatekeeper who is very, very hard to access if we start thinking!

I don't know if you watched the Goop documentaries on Netflix on Psychedelics and Healing? It massively resonated with me as the only way to get past my very strong conscious "thinking" brain is to try and trick it. Otherwise, it is just a brick wall with a massive "no entry" sign that won't let me pass no matter how many hypnosis sessions I have. I'm not suggesting using drugs in this instance! However, I have done a lot of research into how effective psychedelics have been in helping cure addictions which I find incredibly interesting and the prolific usage in tribal ceremonies and folklore (but that's a whole other topic).

I am saying that I know how hard it can be to get past rational thought and to start dealing with what naysayers like to call "pseudoscience" as no one can prove it as it is hidden away in the depths of our truly incredible minds. The best way that I have found to get past the no entry sign is to relax, breathe and shut out all mental shopping lists. When I ask the questions, I just listen for the answers and trust that they are exactly what I am supposed to hear right now rather than questioning them (which is my default setting).

The answers are not set in stone, they will change over time as you evolve, but you've got to start believing in your 'self' for this to be of any help to you. So, just for once, permit yourself to dream a little…

Let's go!

EXERCISE THREE:

1. If I could wear anything, what kind of clothes would I wear/how would I show up?

2. What would my physique be like?

3. What kind of hairstyle would I have?

4. What would my personality be like?

5. How would I take care of myself?

6. What activities would I love to do each day?

7. What food and drink would I consume?

8. What would I do for fun?

9. Where would I go out?

10. Where would I go on holiday?

11. What would make me feel fulfilled?

12. What am I most passionate about?

13. What do I want my legacy to be?

14. What gives me energy?

15. Where would I place my focus right now if I had the choice?

16. How would I like to earn money if money was no object?

17. What would I spend my money on?

18. What things would I stop doing?

19. What things would I start doing?

20. What changes would I start implementing into my life right now if I knew that it was a dead cert that I could become the person that I have just described?

Pow.

I don't know about you but answering those questions is pretty life-affirming. I couldn't even tell my therapist the last time I had experienced happiness, and that's hardly surprising because when I did this exercise on myself, my answers and my reality only overlapped in one or two places.

You may be shocked by your answers and surprised by your dreams and desires. If you wrestle with what you have written or cannot answer them, know this is due to age-old limitations creeping back in.

I will say to you now that for those who have gained a massive understanding of who you are and what your deepest desires are, you need to keep them at the forefront of your mind for the rest of this book. Then we can get your watering system in place to nurture this emerging superwoman.

I want you to read on for those wrestling with your answers and just trust me. I had identified with being a struggling single mum, but my subconscious did not identify with this, which created a massive internal civil war, as Tony Robbins likes to say. But there is a way forward.

For those that have struggled to get clarity, please don't worry. I believe that reading my story will resonate with you, and you will be able to push through the barriers and limitations and go back to that exercise and do it again with a new lease on life. It's not easy creating change. I know that. It's f*cking hard! 'But I also know that it is possible, and essential to your happiness, health, and vitality to set an example to your kids (if you have any and they are still impressionable enough to care).

8

Every choice I make makes me

Now that you have an idea of the woman you are inside, it is a journey of becoming. Spoiler alert - this journey will last a lifetime. But it is the most important journey that you will ever go on, and now that you know that you are in it for the long haul, the best thing you can do is start enjoying the ride because there is nothing else.

This is it. Every day of our lives is a day lived. It shouldn't be passed or tolerated; we should be living. We don't get the days back, and the one thing that is a certainty is that we are all going to die. Morbid but so true. We are not going to be cryogenically frozen. We all need a f*cking rocket up our arses to remind us that we don't have time to waste. This is our only chance to enjoy our lives, and no matter what we do, the worst that can happen is that it's game over.

So with that in mind, it's time to create a really solid values system that supports the woman you truly wish to be. These are effectively your boundaries, your non-negotiables and the things that reinforce your sense of self. Every time you break these boundaries, you undermine your sense of self. The more you do this, the more you erode your self-confidence and lower your self-esteem. Fait acompli. Goodbye, happiness and health.

This is effectively what happened to me. Like I said in the previous chapter, I had identified with being a struggling single mum, but my subconscious did not identify with this. I was too scared to acknowledge the reality that I wanted to create inside of me that was bursting to get out as that involved taking a risk on my 'self 'and rising from a place where I could hide and make excuses for my unhappiness. That created a massive internal civil war inside me as I continued to make choices based on my current reality. So, I continued to undermine myself, making myself more and more unhappy and ill. I went on my merry way, making bad choice after bad choice that didn't align with my values system and eventually succumbing to depression (which I still refused to admit)!

"Every choice I make makes me" (Zig Ziglar) – that's just it!

Let that concept sink in. Every choice we make reinforces who we are to ourselves, and if we aren't making choices that align with our values, we are completely out of whack. To start creating change towards becoming the person you wish to be, you need to make the right choices. To do that, you need to look at your values system associated with your desires to create complete alignment in how you wish to live (and I tell you what, when you are in alignment, the magic truly happens)! This is called intentional living.

If you are anything like me, you inherently have a very strong values system that you just haven't solidified, and you are willing to bend all over the shop to make others happy and appear less demanding! It's called people-pleasing. When your values are compromised, you are compromising your 'self'.

I spent nearly 30 years compromising myself by going against my values system. That's a lot of pain to inflict on your 'self'. It's not something you can heal overnight (believe me, I thought I could)! And your 'self' gets to the point where it doesn't like you anymore. It doesn't want to work for you anymore, and it decides that it's no longer gonna be of service to you as you never take its advice, so it quits. You bent it so far away from itself that it breaks. You become a shell of your former self. Ouch.

You can have all of the best intentions in the world, but if you prioritise others' happiness over your own self, then you are going to end up the broken one. You need to find a compromise between being selfish and being selfless. If you can't hear what your 'self' is saying to you, that's one thing. But if you listen to it and then ignore it or do the complete opposite, that's self-sabotage, and it's not healthy, and it's a horrible place to be. It's like the age-old adage; "you can lead a horse to water, but you can't make it drink". If you continue to ignore your 'self' you will die of thirst.

Establishing strong values as stakes in the ground to support your sense of self so that you can nurture her again creates a solid base to grow from so that you can start making the right decisions which are in complete alignment with your 'self'. Without a strong values system, we are ships being tossed around by the storm in the night. You can have the best intentions in the world, but without any backup to support them, you are screwed. And the storms will come. That's life. But without the storms, we wouldn't appreciate the beauty of the sunshine. There must be contrast in life for us to have the experience.

Being in alignment with your intuition, desires, and

values makes you powerful. It's the most powerful state that you can reside in. It's like getting three lemons lining up on the fruit machine and hitting the jackpot. It is the essence of who you are, and it allows you a platform to springboard from to reach for the stars. No one has the exact same DNA fit of these as you, and that's where your absolute magic lies.

I spent so long doing what other people told me I "should' do because I was basically in a desperate situation and had no other choice. I lived with alarm bells going off around me 24/7 for a good few years. It was frightening and incredibly draining on my body and mind. All that happened was the reinforcement of how I identified with myself as being in a desperate situation. I made really bad choices that reflected other people's opinions of what I should be doing, which compounded and compounded until I didn't know whether I wanted to live a life like that anymore. I was so out of alignment with my 'self'. The stress made me chronically ill, and I hated the person I was. I succumbed to complete darkness. Not just once but several times.

It was hard to acknowledge the place that I was in. I felt that my children deserved a better mum. I wanted to quit. Life felt utterly hopeless. I was drowning trying to keep a roof over our heads, living out of alignment with my values and who I knew that I was underneath all the sh*t. I couldn't understand why I would want to live through this anymore. It was too painful. Just keeping myself alive felt like an insurmountable task. It would be easier to go to sleep and not wake up. That's a pretty desperate situation to be in, and most people looking in from the outside would see me and think that I had it all going on. I didn't want to make anyone feel awkward or let on how much of a failure I thought I was. My programming covered the pain.

So I implore you to address your values system and then shove that stake in the ground like your life depends on it because it does. You must live by these values. They are your infrastructure and will ensure that you always make the right decisions. Nobody knows the actual answers to everything; we are all just getting through by the seat of our pants but having these boundaries and stakes in the ground will help you navigate life so that the scenery on the journey is the stuff you want to see. Easier said than done, I know.

Okay, so let's start by approaching this very simply and look at what a "value" is anyway? According to psychologists Barb Markway and Celia Ampel in The Self-Confidence Workbook, values "are the principles that give our lives meaning and allow us to persevere through adversity."

This resonates so strongly with me because it was only when I started living by my values in line with my desires and intuition that I found hope again. I found the motivation to get back up again when I was knocked flat, which ultimately led me to write this book. I have done an awful lot of road-testing of different routes to happiness. Each time I failed on a new route, I would evaluate what went wrong, what I could take from the experience, and how to improve upon it to implement on the next road test. Failing fast became the best option because it meant that I learnt a lot in a short space of time!! It was pretty painful, but it paid off. I quickly learned everything that I wasn't willing to compromise on.

I believe that living a happy life is the key to happiness (no shit, sherlock). When you are doing things you hate just to earn a buck, you erode your self-worth. I was no longer willing to make money "at all costs" because it cost me to sell my soul to the devil effectively (although I did consider high class escorting when money was particularly tight!). My choices were no longer making me happy. They were doing the complete opposite.

Many saw me as being work-shy or lazy or just living in cloud cuckoo land. I am not in the least bit work-shy or lazy, and maybe I do live a bit in cloud cuckoo land but doing stuff that offers me zero fulfilment just isn't my jam anymore. The stuff that I love doing is the stuff that makes ME happy, and it isn't just sitting at a desk all day working for others and living by their rules and values. I want to live a full and exciting life whilst following my heart and set an example to my beautiful girls to do the same!

As I've said before, it's been a risky journey, but as they say, "no risk, no reward", and that journey is entirely different for all of us. Just think of all the different nuances there are out there. It's virtually impossible to find a carbon copy of yourself, but you can find others with similar values, desires and goals, but their intuition will guide them through life differently. You've probably learned a lot of your values from your parents, teachers, religious leaders and society around you. In mid-life, it's easy to get caught up in the goldfish bowl of values that your immediate peer group have and lose the sense of what is meaningful to you personally. 'Keeping up with the Joneses' is a painful trap to fall into and a hard one to extricate yourself from.

If you're anything like me, you may have rebelled against certain values but learned more about your values system through that rebellion. I know that leaving my marriage was predominantly based on my values. They weren't aligned with where I was, and the only way forward was to change my life.

It was not an easy decision by any stretch of the imagination, but I have learned so much about myself since; that I will always value this journey and embrace the pain that I went through to get to where I am now.

Midlife is a great time to re-evaluate your values system. Like I said before, it can be very easy to have unconsciously stepped away from the values that are inherently important to you as you try and juggle the balls whilst spinning the plates and probably standing on one leg. It's just like having a strategy meeting and reminding yourself of what is important to you on the journey of where you are trying to get to.

EXERCISE 4:

Here's a little exercise that you can do to get an idea of where you are at with your values and to begin identifying what is most important to you. Please remember that your values are deeply personal and uniquely yours; they are the things that you consider important and meaningful in the way you choose to live your life. They define your moral purpose in life. You will naturally find yourself drawn to things/people that align with your values, and they will inspire you to act accordingly. (Hence, the reason why we can sometimes strike up meaningful relationships with people when we have only known them for a short time.)

For example, my answers would be:

1. *Nature! Being immersed and connected with it through almost everything that I do*
2. *Honesty, kindness, empathy, philanthropy, adventurous, GSOH*
3. *Honest, kind, empathic, philanthropic, adventurous, GSOH*

Once you have answered those questions, open your mind to where you live by your values and where you are allowing them to be devalued by choosing quick fixes rather than living by the sword. Because life is not perfect, there will be times when all your values simply cannot be met. When this happens, you need to understand which ones are your non-negotiables to guide your decision making at these key times in your life. This should give you a better understanding of who you are and what makes you tick. It can be a real eye-opener and an amazing guiding system once you've taken the time to acknowledge that you have a values system!

1. Think about life in general. What inspires you and makes you feel energised? What MUST you have in your life?

2. Which qualities do you look for in a partner?

3. If you had to summarise yourself in 6 words – what would they be?

9

You but mark 2

'Our self-image defines who we are to ourselves and the world.'

It's not a revelation, but I feel that this is something that a lot of us fail to recognise when fast fashion and fads are the de-rigueur.

I have always loved clothes and accessories. From the early days of giving my Sindy (a Barbie esque doll for those of you who don't know) a Mohawk that I sprayed with metallic paint and unceremoniously pierced her ears; to making my clothes bespoke to me. I would buy second hand Levis 501s from the army surplus stores and dye them different colours. I had a green pair, a blue pair and a pink pair. I loved them because I knew that no one else would have the same. I wore them with the DM boots I had painted with acrylic paints and my mum's handmade knitted cardigan with flowers on over a boy's grey t-shirt. My friends were all wearing Miss Selfridge clothes and Wallabee shoes. I didn't want to blend in. Once, I got sent to the headmaster's office at school for wearing a grey v-neck jumper instead of our regulation black one. That was pretty rebellious for me. I very much wanted to step away from the crowds from a young age. But, as I got older, I conformed more, and I became less brave. I followed the crowd, and I denied my 'self'.

When I decided that I had to find a new and fulfilling career because I couldn't continue with the marketing work, which was draining me so much, I decided to re-train as a personal stylist because I love style and things of beauty. This went similarly to my training to be an interior designer when I was pregnant with my first child. I enjoyed it so much, and I truly believed that I could make a career of it, but it just wasn't enough.

Yes, I could help people with their image and create a beautiful home, but I wanted to help them find themselves first because this is the basis of everything. Suppose you don't address who the person is inside of you and how they want to show up. In that case, you risk creating an avatar based on somebody else that you think will make you happy, but ultimately they won't. Yes, look for inspiration from others but trust that you have the answers.

Self-image really came to the forefront of my mind when I was rationalising the situation I found myself in versus the person I was. I had always been lucky enough to have money to spend on good quality clothes. When I walked away from my financial stability, clothes and accessories were a luxury that I could not afford. I wrestled with the fact that I wouldn't be able to pay to have my highlights done anymore! First world problems and all that.

But it really hit me hard. Was I going to have to change my whole image to align with the situation I found myself in, like I was playing a part? The psychology behind it baffled me. I felt so vain for wanting to still show up as the woman I had been, but my finances no longer reflected that woman through no fault of my own. I felt like an outcast. I was so cross with myself that I couldn't give up these material possessions and just dress in sackcloth and ashes. I read the teachings of buddha to try and make sense of it all. But it was when I was studying for my personal styling course I had the revelation that how we show up in life is unbelievably important. It is how we show who we are inside. It's been this way for centuries.

Let's take Cleopatra, for example. She is pretty much my idol, apart from the murderous and incestuous stuff she got up to. She wore bright green malachite paste on her lower eyelids and a deep blue eye shadow with gold pyrite flecks on her upper eyelids that enhanced her beautiful eyes and protected them from sun damage. She darkened her eyebrows and lengthened her eyelashes using black kohl made from lead sulfide and animal fat. She even wore lipstick, blusher and nail polish made from henna. And why did she do this? She used her cosmetics and her jewellery not just for beauty's sake but for the power it created for her over the men that she drew into her life. By doing this, she became more and more powerful. She was on to something.

On a side note, she also bathed in ass's milk which sounds crazy, but she was way ahead of the game. When milk sours, the lactose converts into lactic acid, which can cause the surface layer of the skin to peel off, leaving new blemish-free skin underneath. How would she even have known that without all the chemical testing on rats undertaken by the beauty industry? She knew it because of her intuition. She understood how nature works for us. Everyone is after these beauty products now. She also made natural perfumes and dabbled in creating baldness remedies, spurred by her relationship with Julius Caesar, who was hair challenged. When this didn't work, she traded him in for Marc Anthony! I like her style. The Egyptians were also amongst the first wearers of established jewellery made from precious metals that showed their status. I mean, not much has changed as we have evolved.

In the same way, our CV represents our career history, a website aesthetic represents a brand, and our self-image represents the person we want to play in life. We are all actors playing ourselves. We get to decide on our costumes and the backdrop for our lives. We are the creators of our reality. You wouldn't go to an interview looking a mess; you want to convey the essence of yourself. Society judges you on how you show up in life; it's as simple as that. You are a walking billboard for your 'self'. To play the game of life, you need to recognise and acknowledge that it is necessary to care for how you interact with others and interact with yourself.

I don't know about you, but if I look like sh*t and I'm wearing clothes that I don't like or align with, I feel crap. I remember a trip to Ibiza that I took with some friends just after I had left my marriage.

I was feeling very quiet and tender. I didn't want to be seen. I took my favourite worn out denim shorts, a couple of nice tops and my flip flops. When we went out in the evenings, my friends got dressed up to the nines. Playsuits, dresses, high heels, hair done, make up on point and strutting their stuff. When we got to the bar, there were loads of girls wearing what I had wanted to wear. I just wanted my shorts and top and flats, but

I let them cajole me into wearing one of their little black dresses. We went out, and I spent the whole night hating myself and hating what I was wearing because it just wasn't me, but I had wanted to conform and be part of the gang. I wouldn't have been out of place. It was an important lesson for me. There is no benefit to conforming to what others want you to be if that isn't who you are inside. I wasn't strong enough back then to embrace myself. Had I done, I would have stood out for being the one who didn't follow the crowd, and I would have been happy - the ultimate goal.

We are all judgemental of each other; we can't help it because our self-image is a form of silent communication. Granted, we aren't all going to look tip-top every minute of every day (I certainly don't, I'm in my PJs by approx. 4.30 most days), but when you look at yourself and like what you see, you certainly feel better about who you are! It would be much easier if we were all naked or in uniform the whole time (it's got my vote), but life isn't like that. It's way too cold for naked in the UK and uniform takes away our ability to self-express and step away from the crowd, which is fun! We are individuals, after all.

Our self-image is an external reflection of our internal intention and thus is beyond important. It is also the one thing that we have complete control over.

EXERCISE 5 – CREATING A STYLE UNIFORM:

With that in mind, I want to do another exercise with you that builds on the first exercise but takes it into a lot more depth. Let's quickly revisit your answers to the first three questions:

Part 1

1. If I could wear anything, what kind of clothes would I wear/how would I show up?

2. What would my physique be like?

3. What hairstyle would I have?

So this is fairly generalistic but gives a topline overview of where you want to be. What I want you to do now is get really specific with this. I want you to think about who you want to be underneath the weight of life and start creating a 'signature style' that is effortless and 100% emulates you. To make this easier, let's begin by thinking about the following questions:

Part 2

Who would I like to emulate?

There's no need to re-create the wheel! Think of someone you admire; it can be a friend or a famous person (from the present or the past), and it can be more than one person. I want you to think of someone you really feel aligned with when it comes to how they present themselves and look at what they are wearing. E.g. I wanted to be Elle McPherson with a side of Patsy from Ab Fab, but I looked to Alexa Chung for style inspiration!

Part 3

What do you do with your days, and therefore what different 'wardrobes' do you need to suit your lifestyle?

E.g. I do sport each day, so a sports kit is very important to me. I also have two young kids, so I need to have clothes to run around a muddy park and go for walks. I also need smarter clothes for work meetings and going out. Seasonal wardrobes for the summer holidays are important to me because summer is my heyday!

It's easy to see how overwhelming our wardrobe requirements can be just from asking ourselves these questions. What we want to do is simplify and refine this as much as possible. I promise that it is easier to manage once we know what we need!

Part 4:

Next, ask yourself the following questions:

- What colours do I like to wear? *It is not about which colours' suit' you but what colours lift you up. If you are a monochrome person, then you are winning! If you could reduce the colour ways in your wardrobe to 4 or 5 maximum, what would they be?*

- Do I like to wear patterns or plain, slogans or pictures etc.? *Make a decision and stick to it!*

- What brands do I align with? *Are there any particular shops/brands you really like that fit you well and you feel good wearing? Narrowing down where you shop can make life a whole lot easier.*

- Do I value comfort over looks? *If you are anything like me, comfort is essential. I cannot wear anything that isn't comfortable. In my 20's, yes, I didn't give a shit. Now I can't deal with it!*

- Heels or flats? *Heels are for special occasions, not the muddy park! There is a place for both in most wardrobes, but I am much more prone to wearing flats these days.*

- Is there one item of clothing or an accessory that I love that can become the basis of my signature style? *For example, a gold watch, a hair accessory, a bow, sunglasses, a handbag, a type of footwear, a trouser length.*

- Where am I happiest investing money in my wardrobe? *Which items make me happiest? Is it shoes, handbags, sunglasses, accessories, coats etc.?*

- What am I missing that I really need that would make me feel good about myself? *Are you missing a smart coat? Or a good pair of trainers? Or a quality handbag? Where are you underselling yourself?*

- What items of my clothing are junky and could do with upgrading? *If you are anything like me, it is your underwear drawer!!*

Upgrading your wardrobe has a massive impact on your overall self-esteem. Investing in the basics for all of your lifestyle needs will make a huge difference to your ability to be prepared for all that life has to throw at you and save you time in the long run. I can't impress you enough with how life-changing having a capsule wardrobe of quality over quantity items is. It makes you feel good, saves space, saves money, massively reduces overwhelm when it comes to getting ready each day, and no more time wasted on shopping or fast fashion! I will go into this more in a later chapter, but positive luxury really is the way forward to living a fulfilled and happy life.

All the power is in your hands when it comes to your self-image. You get to make the choices. If you can't be bothered, that will be reflected in how you show up. You are effectively saying to your 'self' that you aren't bothered about her and saying to others that you aren't bothered about your appearance, and maybe that's your thing. I'm not judging anyone; I want you to recognise that the way you show up in life is valid for all the reasons I gave above.

I don't want to spend hours on my appearance and in the shops, quite the opposite. I wear very little makeup. I eat well to keep my complexion and hair healthy. I keep my body in good shape, which is my most important representation of myself. My favourite outfit is a tan. I have a capsule wardrobe of quality items that reflect my values. I wear the same kind of thing every day, pretty much but in various formats. It is my style uniform, and I love the ease it offers me in life. It takes very little energy to get dressed each day. It takes up very little room, which is essential for me. Packing is so much easier, and when I look at my clothes, I genuinely love them.

My favourite outfit is my black tie outfit. It consists of a dress that I bought years ago from ASOS. It is bright and garish, but there is something about the colours and the fit and the collar that I truly love. It emulates me. I wear it with a pair of kitten heel gold sandals and my small black Mulberry handbag. I don't care that it's been seen before. I have worn it to my school summer ball three times. Every time I wear it, I get comments on how amazing it is. What's the point in constantly trying to change it up?

Find your happy place when it comes to your clothes (or armour), and stick with it. It is how the clothes make you FEEL, not what others think. If they make you feel good, then you are winning. If they don't make you feel good, this is perhaps an aspect of your life that you need to address because they can make you feel like a million dollars and give you confidence that you may currently be lacking. Remember to dress for the part that you want to play in life. Personal style is, first and foremost, accepting who you are.

10

Accept it, change it or bloody well leave it!

Okay, so now the shit is getting real. It has been my mantra since I re-started my life. Accept it, change it, or bloody well leave it, but stop f*cking complaining about the same thing repeatedly and never addressing it.

Have you heard the story about the guy who walks down the road and falls into a hole? I can't remember it exactly, but it goes something like this.

A guy walks down a road on his way to work and falls down a hole. It's a pain in the arse, but he climbs back out and carries on. The next day he walks down the same road and falls back down the same hole. Again, he dusts himself off and carries on, but he does the same thing the next day. So, he thinks he must remember to avoid that hole and go round it but lo and behold, the next day, in his haste, he totally forgets about avoiding the hole and falls into it again.

No matter how hard he tries, he can't seem to avoid that hole. It's really beginning to get to him as he can't seem to avoid that hole no matter what he does. One day he remembers to walk around it, but he's so busy being proud of himself that he falls straight back into it again the next day.

So do you know what he decides to do? (And no, it's not getting in touch with the Highways Agency) He chooses to walk a different road.

Think about what you can accept, change or leave. If something makes you unhappy, you are better off changing it than not taking action and letting it drain you of your energy and happiness. Stop trying to be someone else. You can't run from yourself. You've been running for too long. It's time to sit with yourself, make friends and offer the nurture and support you aren't necessarily getting from elsewhere.

I have lost a lot of friends because of my opinions and perspective and just the way I lead my life. I have to let them go. They weren't my people. Don't listen to other people's opinions of you, and don't try and justify your life. You are the captain of your ship, steering the boat. Keep your eye to the horizon and readjust your compass only where you feel it is necessary. When you are so far adrift from where you need to be, the only choice you have is to look inside for guidance.

There have been some key things for me in my life that I have changed because I couldn't accept or leave them. The first was having my ears pinned back in my 20s. Throughout school and my working career, people endlessly teased me for having sticking out ears. I got called Dark Crystal (I hope you guys are old enough to remember that, but if not, google it), gremlin, bat ears etc. I felt so ugly. I was a pretty girl, but my ear situation made me feel ridiculous and constantly embarrassed. At school, I created endless hairstyles to cover my ears (I mostly looked like a nun). At uni, I started to stick my ears back with plasters. I would then have to keep them covered so that no one could see the plasters.

Sometimes the plasters would pop off whilst I was out. It was like being Cinderella at the stroke of midnight, and I turned back into the real ugly version of me. I kept away from boys because I didn't want anyone seeing my plasters or discovering the truth of the monstrosity that I felt that I was underneath. I felt like a fraud, but I couldn't deal with the truth. In the film 'There's something about Mary', I became like Warren. If anyone came anywhere near my ears, I would instinctively punch them! It took over my life, it ate away at my self-worth and eventually, I got them pinned back in my mid-20s when a burst eardrum meant that I had to have an ear op anyway. I jokingly asked my surgeon if he could pin my ears back whilst he was there, and that's exactly what he did. If only I had looked into it sooner. I could have saved myself years of pain. Tbh the mental scarring is still there, I find it hard to look at myself, but I am becoming more accepting. They are the least of my worries now.

Another thing that really bothered me about my appearance was my crooked teeth. They weren't crooked in a cute way. They were a mess! I found it hard to clean between them because they were all over each other. I desperately wanted to get them straightened, but it felt way too vain and frivolous. By some randomness, just after my 40th birthday, I hit my front tooth really hard with a glass that I was drinking from. It was already slightly crooked, but it seemed to be more so after I hit it, and it hurt like hell. I went to the dentist, and he told me that the impact had caused my tooth to twist slightly. Combining that with the amount that I was clenching my teeth at night from stress was causing it to twist even more, and if I left it, there was a chance that the root would break. It would then turn grey or fall out in the worst case!

WTAF. I was recently divorced. I had just turned

40. I had two little kids. I could not cope with losing my f*cking front tooth as well! So I used the last bit of money I had to pay the deposit on my Invisalign treatment. It took just under a year. It was miraculous. I loved how just creating a small amount of space and the tiniest of movements over a long period of focused time could create such incredible results!

It wasn't easy. If you've had Invisalign, you know that you are constantly teeth cleaning. You get to the point where you can't be arsed to eat because you must keep taking your retainers in and out, but it's an excellent way to stop you snacking! I loved the change that I could create through focus and intention, and that's where my life by design interest started to pique. If I could achieve that…what else could I achieve through small changes over a long period? It's like the domino effect. It starts slowly, but the momentum of pushing over that first domino sets off a chain reaction that gets stronger and stronger and faster and faster.

Once I had had my teeth straightened, I felt like I could smile again without trying to cover my teeth. I felt proud of them. I could clean easily between each tooth. They made me feel good, and feeling good is the goal. Yes, it may sound vain, but it isn't if it is bothering you so much. We all want to feel good, and it is so worth changing the stuff that you can't accept.

Or you can leave it and let it eat away at you. Funnily enough, I had 'excuses' for doing each with both of those examples. I needed those to almost allow me to do them. I wouldn't have permitted myself otherwise. Knowing what I know now, I wouldn't need an 'excuse' or permission to feel good about myself. Let my story be your permission.

My biggest accept it/change it or leave it lesson has been my marriage and subsequent divorce. I tried accepting where I was, but it made me very ill. I tried to change things, but that didn't work, and in the end, I had to leave. I had covered all bases. It was by no means an easy decision. It blew up my life. The ripple effect is strong, and I have had to take radical responsibility for my actions.

I hope it will remain the hardest decision I have ever had to make. I don't think I can do anything bigger than that. But it will also be the decision that changed my life, and I hope that it inspires you to change the course of your life by making hard decisions.

I'm not suggesting getting divorced! I'm just saying, 'don't stay in situations that don't fuel you.' Remember that you always have a choice. Accept it. Change it. OR leave it.

EXERCISE 6:

Time for a bit of journaling (I think I probably hit my bullshit bingo with some of you by saying that!)

I want you to write down all the things bothering you right now. The things that aren't making you happy and weighing on your mind. Write them out as a list. Go through the list, and next to each gripe, I want you to write down whether it falls into the accept it change it or leave it.

i.e.

My relationship with my partner isn't great ...change it
I'm not enjoying my job at all anymore ...leave it
I don't like the way my body looks nake ...change it
Social media pisses me off but is essential for work ...accept it
My relationship with my daughter is waning ...change it
My parents/friends don't understand me ...accept it
I hate my home ...change it/leave it

Etc. Give yourself a choice.

11

Create some space to flourish

By chance, I discovered a modern approach to sustainability through all of the absolute bullsh*t that I went through. It was a prime example of how there are such rewarding lessons even in the darkest of times - if you just take a moment to find the light. I know it's a major cliché, but it's that or despair.

Since leaving my marriage meant leaving my family home with nowhere to go and no funds to pay for a home, and no idea wtf I was going to do, I had to do a major, major de-clutter as I left life as I once knew it. The beautiful five-bedroom, 4,000 square foot barn conversion with annexe and the triple garage was out, and I would be homeless until the next step presented itself.

This meant that I had to clarify what I wanted to keep because it all had to go into storage. I somehow needed to pay for that storage, and money wasn't forthcoming. I remember getting my sisters over and asking them to just throw everything from the garages and storage into the skip unless it looked valuable or sentimental. I didn't have the time or the headspace to get all Marie Kondo and pick up each item to see if it resonated with me. I binned everything that seemed cumbersome and didn't fit my new life. All the old love letters went too! I was brutal in my approach. I got rid of all my beautiful shoes and clothes from my working life, thinking I would never need them again. Nothing was safe. I was on a mission to lift the load that weighed so heavily over me.

Having to store possessions was a major drain on my finances and mental resources. I remember spending so much time in our big house trying to work out how to build more storage for all our ever-increasing possessions and clothes. When I had finished, I truly felt like I had lifted a huge load from my life. Left behind was only a small van load of belongings (not including bulky furniture), all of which mattered to me. Every item was something that I cherished or was entirely necessary. I was hooked on having less. It never occurred to me before to get rid of stuff instead of building more storage!

Now, if the house feels too full, I de-clutter. When

my home life and environment are taken care of, I feel calmer and more creative and generally much happier. It reminded me of one of the happiest times when I travelled the world with just my backpack and very few possessions. I felt free. Having less makes you feel free. It also means that when you pass on (aka die), your kids/family won't have to go through tonnes of stuff and feel obliged to hold onto any of your stuff because there really isn't any. You have done it all for them. I continuously keep on top of it, doing audits of what I need and removing the stuff we no longer need, which is ongoing as the kids grow. I try and pass this lesson onto them, too, as we release the items that we no longer need or love and give them to charity or sell them on so that they can save up for something new that they really want. I must do this as I live in a small house with very little storage space and that's fine by me. I love living lean. What I have I love, and what I don't have, I don't need. This gives me the space to flourish and breathe.

When I shop for clothes and accessories (which I love btw), I invest. I buy for longevity, and I buy as little as possible. I get the things I love the most; I save up for what I want. I ensure that I have a simple capsule wardrobe so that everything works together and will fit in my cupboard and the overhead locker when I fly with Easyjet! It is a blessing not having space as space so often gets filled. I rarely (if ever) impulse purchase unless I truly love something.

It is the same for interiors. I absolutely love creating an environment that makes me happy (hence why I trained in interior design). To achieve that result, I use the basics of feng shui and biophilic design. They are naturally within me, and I find it joyful to create a beautiful and functional home for my children and me. The major benefit of being alone is that I don't have to get my décor ideas approved by anyone or work out how to include their inherited stuffed pheasant in the overall design scheme.

When I first moved into my new home after getting divorced, the décor was not to my liking, and there is no benefit in being in a space that makes you feel low. So, I created an ambience that I felt uplifted by with some simple, inexpensive changes such as painting all the walls and doors white, painting my kitchen cupboards, replacing the tiles and work surface (with a £100 fake granite one) and throwing in a load of plants, candles, crystals and artwork. I didn't have the finances to do much, but what I did made a difference in my mindset. Never underestimate the power of your surroundings and immediate environment. There is beauty in the most inexpensive objects, such as a plant or a beautiful shell you collected from the beach. Nature does provide for us, and I love to look around and remember the story behind everything that I own. Although I still find it hard to actually light my candles as they will burn out... working on that one!

Another major overhaul was my beauty regime. I stripped out everything with chemicals and replaced complicated skincare regimes with simple, natural regimes that worked. I got rid of all of my old make-up and, with the help of a make-up artist and friend, simplified my make-up requirements with something for daytime and nighttime (if I ever go out)! This saved on space; it also improved my skin health and bank balance.

I also got rid of all the food products and kitchen paraphernalia that I didn't need and didn't fit with my new lifestyle. (Now I just eat the kid's crisps and chocolate). My exercise regime is structured to fit seamlessly within my days (running, weight training and yoga/pilates) unless I'm on a mission which is most of the time!!

I didn't stop there. I de-cluttered my emails, friends on Facebook (!), subscriptions to newsletters, photos, apps on my phone and my Christmas card list. Everything that I could to simplify and detox my life to give me more space to flourish. I learnt that having less is absolutely more. Buying once but buying better is so rewarding, and the less stuff I have, the more life I get to live. Effectively it is positive luxury which is a way to live that improves our wellbeing, mental health and sense of self. It also reduces overwhelm, saves money and provides sustainability for the planet and your energy levels. What could be better than that?

Once you've finished this book, my aim is that you will be able to de-clutter your life in alignment with what you want from it. Not just blindly chucking stuff in a skip (although that was 100% necessary at the time for me). I used the Marie Kondo "Life-Changing Magic of Tidying Up" book as I refined my desires, but it was only when I truly knew what I wanted from life and how I wanted to show up that this was an effective route for me. If you try and do this when you don't know who you are or where you are going, it is like the blind leading the blind. I still regret giving my peacock-coloured Reiss high heels to charity, but that was pre-Marie, so I won't pin that on her.

12

It's all about energy flow bro

Okay, so this book is effectively about how intrinsically linked your happiness is to your health and wellbeing. The message, in a nutshell, is that suffering is not the answer unless you have chosen to sacrifice yourself for a higher calling, e.g. to become a nun or a school teacher.

I have decided to sacrifice a straightforward life where I conform to the norm to test my theories on myself to see if they work, and that makes me happy. I am my own guinea pig, and through doing this, I can then report back to you guys with authority on what worked and what didn't work. I drive fast at brick walls to see how best to get through (metaphorically speaking), and when I fail, I tend to my wounds and rebuild. I try new tactics such as changing my speed, getting a new car, training more, looking at my fuel and working on my mindset to overcome the fear of hurting myself and damaging my vehicle!

My point is that your energy levels are highly dependent on living in alignment with yourself and doing what makes you happy. No matter what those things are and how frightening they may seem. I know this only too well. My energy levels were seriously low for 15 years or so. Adrenal fatigue got me from the years of stress of living out of alignment and not taking care of myself (something I have made massive changes to now). A big part of boosting my energy levels was working out what lights my energy up rather than how to simply fuel it. Like the plant analogy from earlier, we need more than just nutrients to thrive.

I had very much got into the mindset that it was solely what I put into my body which determined what I got out of it, which caused me to be pretty obsessive about nutrition. It led to more stress over eating super well, and this became the be-all and end-all, and that ain't healthy even though what I was putting into myself was healthy…does that make sense? It's not about what you put in/do necessarily. It's about how you 'feel' about what you are doing. The placebo effect is a massive thing.

The placebo effect is proven; it is a scientific fact. If you 'believe' something is true, it will be (which is what teachers like Joe Dispenza teach us). But (and this was a massive eye-opener for me) what you can't do is override your beliefs and create a placebo result that you want! That is a delusion. I know because I have tried! I have tried to do stuff out of alignment with myself and convince my brain that it is good for me because I want it to be the right answer when I know full well that it isn't. The placebo effect only works if every cell in your body believes to the same degree.

You can eat all your five a day and still be unhappy. It will help, but it's not the answer in itself. To be happy, healthy and fulfilled, you need to do the stuff that makes YOU feel good all the way through. Not the stuff that everyone else tells you will make you feel good. Only you know the juicy stuff that lights you up, which is also part of your fuel. It activates your energy. Nutrition is a part of this, but it's not the whole.

I gave up doing so many things that I loved because they felt frivolous (and I couldn't afford a lot of them), but I kept them prioritised because I learnt that they were my 'activating activities'. As I consciously created my lifestyle, I learned how I responded to different activities from work, exercise, social events and everything in between. I paid particular attention to how they made me FEEL (something it had never occurred to me to do as I just thought I had to suck everything up). I discovered that if I did something that I didn't enjoy, I would drain my energy reserves super fast (which I couldn't afford to do as they were in short supply). Whereas if I did something that I did enjoy, it would give me a massive boost. I had to learn to manage my energy flow effectively to get the best out of myself.

"Working hard for something we don't care about is called stress. Working hard for something we love is called passion." Simon Sinek

It's fairly fucking obvious, right but so many of us dismiss this idea as impractical. Who am I to be happy and be seen to enjoy myself? What kind of crazy is this that I could possibly enjoy myself? Everyone will judge me as a very shallow person if I appear happy when so much sh*t is happening around me. Who am I to choose work that fulfils me when I just need to earn money?

Those are the kind of things that I used to say to myself over and over, and I am sure you have been there too. There's the guilt of being at home and enjoying life whilst your partner commutes to work, the guilt of going out with friends at the weekend and living it up and leaving the kids. The guilt of saying no to work that doesn't align when you are desperate for money. We feel that we have to be martyrs or else we will be ostracised, and also we feel like we don't have any other choice. Who are we to choose what we do and how we live? Surely we have to do what we have to do and play the cards dealt?

The answer to that is yes and no. We must play the cards but the ones that will win us the game.

Ultimately this is what living is about - doing the things that boost your energy and put a smile on your face rather than the things that drain you and burn energy fast and make you miserable. These activating activities are different for everyone. As I discovered in my search for happiness, we need to ensure that we build them into our lives to give us a boost and balance out the mundane.

"All work and no play makes Jack a dull boy."

On that note, I spent a long time doing work that didn't fulfil me after I left my marriage; I had to do anything to earn money. Overnight I became the provider for myself and my kids, having not worked for six years. All this did was drain me. It drained every last drop of energy I had left, and I reached the stage where I could not go on. I asked the doctor if she could sign me off work with stress, and she willingly obliged. It was completely pointless as, at the time, I was a freelancer, and if I didn't work, I didn't get paid, but mentally I felt better!

I tried every job, from freelance marketing to social media to copywriting. I worked at a local venue, tried lifestyle coaching to personal styling, to taking a job as a project manager in a design studio. I lasted a day there until I realised that the work and my life just didn't marry up. I considered every standard career option, but none seemed to fit with how I wanted to live my life and the care levels I wanted to give my children. They were all out of alignment with my values and desires, and hence none of them activated my energy. At my lowest point, high class escorting seemed like the best option! Desperate times require desperate measures! Let's move on quickly!

To create a good energy flow, we need to understand the science behind energy and how we can relate it to human beings. Fortunately, this is pretty easy once we recognise that we are all electrical beings. Everything in the universe is made of energetic cells with chemical reactions constantly at work, and we are no different. Why would we be? We are part of nature. Once you are down with that, the rest is simple.

For every action, there is a reaction. A positive and a negative that we can align with the yin and the yang. That's how energy works, and that's how our lives work. There are two sides to every coin, and there is a catch 22 to every choice we make: the light and the dark. We can't have one without the other. While diametrically opposing each other, these positives and negatives are essential for energy flow and thus growth throughout our cosmos.

To create energy within us, we must include activating activities in our lives (the positives), but these will often come at a price (the negative). Negatives may be a physical price or the price of having to give something else up to include them in our lives. E.g. going for a run in the morning for half an hour might mean not being able to work and earn X amount of money in that half an hour each morning. However, I am very much of the opinion that you will make up for that 'lost' work time somewhere else in your life from the energy flow that you have gained if it activates your energy.

I became 'Jack the dull boy' for a long time. I thought my only way forward in life was to strip out all of the frivolity of what made me happy, as I couldn't afford the time, money or attention that I put to them. I was f*cking miserable. But I was in good shape. I am also an introverted-extrovert or "ambivert." I find crowds really overwhelming, and I am a bit of a loner. I like to have time by myself to unwind the knots in my mind. But I equally love people, the right people, though, which has been a big learning for me. I can go for long periods on my own, but then I get to the point where I need to be around others to pick up on their energy like I'm recharging my battery from their resources.

During the lockdown, I really felt it. I'm so used to living a fairly solitary lifestyle as a single mum that I actually enjoyed not having the FOMO that I'm used to, and permission not to go out was awesome. But sometimes, I felt so flat, and it was only when I met up with others that I felt like I was recharging. I realised that I needed to be close to other beings to pick up on their energy. This really demonstrated how connected we are to each other and how much we need each other.

Social media has made this much more accessible, but (as with everything) there are negative aspects to it. When I felt good in myself and was in a 'high vibe' state, I noticed that it compelled others to ask me how I got there. When I shared what I did to get into that state (i.e. my activating activities), I permitted them to do something that they may have felt they weren't entitled to do to feel better! It works the converse way too. If I am feeling low and I see someone on a high, I want to know what they are having so I can have some of it too! That's the beauty of life and sharing our experiences.

Activating our energy flow positively is vital for our quality of life. Anger, frustration, resentment and bitterness are all significant drains. But you can convert them into a positive if you can create the awareness to capture that energy and channel it into something that fulfils you. Rest is key. I have read so many self-help books written by men, and they are all about push, push, push…never give up! I tried that route, and I quickly burnt out. I'm a midlife mum with raging hormones, endless responsibilities and a million things going on at once and pushing through means burning out. I have learned the hard way through my adrenal fatigue that rest is essential. It doesn't mean that you are quitting or have lost focus; it means that you are preparing for the next push. Athletes do not train all of the time; they have rest days. As an athlete, you are almost always on; every day is a race.

You must learn to get rid of energy drains (which we'll go into in a later chapter), light your fires through activating activities, and discover your best ways to recharge your battery and sit and rest without guilt!

EXERCISE 7: – COME ON, BABY, LIGHT YOUR FIRE:

In this exercise, we are building on your answers from Exercise 3. I want you to think about activities that make you happy, energetic and write them down in a list. I then want you to write down what it is about them that makes you happy.

Then, I want you to write down the activities that help you relax/recharge (effectively create latent energy) and why/how they do this for you.

I am going for full disclosure below, where I have detailed mine. However, this list continues to evolve and is by no means exhaustive. My activating energies are random, and some of them I would have been embarrassed to share before because I would worry about being classed as a dumb blonde, but I'm really over caring about what others think, so here are mine:

Things that make me happy , activate my energy and why:

- Going for a run in nature – *it's the being outdoors bit for me. I don't really do treadmills anymore; I love being outside and seeing the countryside and life at work. I don't run to compete with anyone or anything, least of all myself; I run purely to experience the joy of being able to run and to revel in my surroundings. I will stop to take in the view and smell the metaphorical roses. If I am tired, I will walk. Running is like a meditation for me, but also it is a chance to multi-task without the drain of a multi-task (as multi-tasking is bad for you!). It allows me to reconnect with nature, move my way through any challenges/ tricky emotions in my mind and keep my body active. It's a yes from me.*
- Eating amazing food that looks beautiful and nourishes me. *Just the DNA of high quality, whole foods make me feel good. I feel so grateful to be able to eat as close to nature as I do. I am always blown away by the miracle of how it provides for us through its nutrients; food is medicine!*
- Sunbathing and sunbeds (I am tanorexic) - *yes, I have sunbeds because they make me feel so good, which overrides my negative. I believe that the sun is a positive in my life. I won't let the adverse side effects take the jam out of this doughnut for me. No wrinkles or never having the sunshine on my face? I know which one I will pick every time... doesn't mean I love the wrinkles, but I chose them and having a tan makes me feel indestructible, and the Vit D from the sunshine is essential.*
- Having my hair blow-dried – *makes me feel polished and luxurious. I feel a million dollars when I step out of*

that salon, so it is a perfect way to really activate my energy for something where I need to be high vibe, man!

- Getting dressed up – *I am a comfort all the way kinda gal, so I am investing more in my loungewear and sports gear (basically all elastic waists). But I love getting dressed up with heels and jewels for an event, it feels so good, and I feel powerful.*
- Doing something creative – *where to start with this? I love sewing, knitting, embroidery, crafting, making, drawing, writing (in particular self-expression), designing, interior design… the list and the possibilities are endless. But for a long time, these things were nice to have, but I didn't have the time. Now I make the time.*
- Exercising – *any exercise that I am feeling at the time, sometimes I'm all about the stretch. Sometimes it's the strength; it constantly evolves and changes as I love trying new things. I truly loved the Pilates reformer, then I gave pole dancing a go and was hooked, but then I moved on to boxing! Exercise gets those endorphins going, and it is something that we can all do at no cost and quickly see results. I love the challenge, but there are so many things to try and so little time! I'm like a kid in a sweetshop when it comes to ways to work out.*
- Any outdoor pursuits or adventures (ideally with like-minded others) – *love an outing or an escapade. Always more entertaining when something goes wrong.*
- Creating memories and feeding off of other people's energy. *I'm a thalassophile through and through.*
- Being by or in the sea or any body of water (that doesn't have chemicals in it). *Maybe it's the minerals present in the air, the calming nature of the water, or*

perhaps it's the ocean's vastness. Maybe she's born with it. What I can't do anymore is chlorine pools or hot tubs full of chemicals unless it's essential! They wreck my skin; I can taste it, my hair goes brittle just looking at it, and it brings me zero joy.

- Playing tennis or any other racquet sports – *I love tennis, padel tennis, squash, badminton, and golf (driving range only). They are so pleasurable, and it's fun!*
  I am not competitive at sports; I just like playing (like a child).
- Discovering new places, going on holidays – *um, my nickname used to be Judith Chalmers (so that probably tells you everything you need to know). I love a holiday, but now I am very intentional about where I go and what I spend my money on. I am all about barefoot luxury; I don't like ostentatious. I want to be close to nature. Nudist resorts will be the next big thing, I guarantee. Location is everything.*
- Listening to music – *I use different music genres depending on my mood, but music can be so powerful. It can take you back to a place and a time in the past which brings back great memories. In my twenties, I went sky diving in Australia with my dad and friends. I have a sky diving video (of course) (omg, I said video! It is a video I had transferred to a DVD! Wow, I need to upload it somewhere!) That video has your stereotypical skydive music from Oasis' Champagne Supernova' to 'Jump' by Van Halen. I play those songs whenever I feel low and want to up the ante.*

Things that make me happy , activate my energy and why:

Things that make me happy and charge my battery:

- Going for walks in nature – *I love being outdoors (if you haven't noticed), and I love movement. If I need to recharge and haven't the energy for a run, I walk. After leaving my marriage, I spent my spare time walking and listening to Louise Hay for a good five years. My life had fallen apart, and I was frightened. My focus had gone, and I didn't know what to do. I was pretty broken but walking and processing the emotions were my saviour. I still love to walk as often as I can. Sometimes I will listen to motivational music, words etc. Twice a day is my usual benchmark! Sometimes I will simply listen to the birds and appreciate my life.*
- Beauty/wellbeing treatments: massage, reflexology, facials, reiki, cranial-sacral therapy, pedicure and manicure. *Basically, anything that involves touch and releases stress from my body These treatments feel great, but they also do great things and help me relax and recharge.*
- I love the inspiration that I get from the stories of listening to inspiring podcasts, watching films about people overcoming challenges or watching extreme sports. *The human spirit is truly indomitable, and I zone out of my head.*
- Going to the cinema – I love films and the pre-views. I love being totally engrossed in one thing and not having any other distractions. I love an excuse to sit down.
- Reading – *it's not exactly rockstar, but it's a chance to relax, rebalance and re-program my mind and zone out depending on what I'm reading. I love a bit of trashy*

romance as much as I love a Pulitzer Prize winner. I can read books that I love over and over again. They take me away from my life to faraway lands. I am also the Bridget Jones of self-help. I reckon I could open a book shop with the number of self-help books I have read, so who better to write this book!

- Being in bed/sleeping – *is one of my favourite places. I literally love my bed! Sleep is so important to me. I reckon I need 8 hours of sleep a night. I am no Maggie Thatcher. I truly love sleeping well to get up and seize the day! I put thought into my bedroom environment. No TVs or electronics for me, no lights other than my SAD light (for my seasonal affective disorder, of course)! My room is a place of calm, tranquillity and beauty. My mattress is just so; my sheets are a high thread count cotton; I will not scrimp on a place where I spend so much quality time! I'm a highly sensitive person, like the princess in the "Princess and the Pea" story. I reckon I would be able to feel a pea under ten mattresses; it's bloody annoying, but it's my superpower, and now I am so self-aware. I see and feel everything. I can literally sniff things out.*
- Sex /Personal pleasure - *this is something that I have re-discovered in my 40's post-divorce. I enjoy the pleasure and release of sex more than ever. It's a way of completely switching off and being in the moment, I feel good for it, and it is a great way to recharge. The power of the human touch is indescribable, and an orgasm works wonders for your health. Sex is a bit like going to the gym; you quite often don't want to, and you might force yourself to go, but it is rather enjoyable, and you wonder why you don't do it more often. This is something to consider when you*

are too tired and can't be arsed. It also allows you to reconnect with your partner (ideally)! Sex is basically good for your health, so try and make an effort to include it more often in your lifestyle.

Things that make me happy and charge my battery and why:

I hope my list with my 'why's' has inspired you to write your list, including your 'why's'. I remember not knowing what activated my energy and how to manage its flow. Through time and profound self-awareness, I have created this list, so don't be hard on yourself if it doesn't come easily. (Remember that when my therapist asked me the last time I had been happy, I couldn't find anything to report.)

Being conscious that activating activities are a thing and letting yourself 'feel' how things sit with you will help you build this. Then you can implement these activities into your life knowing that although they may seem "frivolous" and "non-essential", they are actually serving your best interests, i.e. making you happy and thus improving your overall wellbeing and ability to function: less Jack, more thrill.

13

How to work your earth wire

So you may be wondering wtf I am on about, so I will explain to you. It is something that I am super passionate about, and it is so, so important for our wellbeing whilst also being unbelievably simple and so totally overlooked! Have you heard of 'grounding'?

It has become the latest buzzword, but I'm not sure that the reasoning behind its importance is clear. You can view 'Grounding' as a way of centring yourself and connecting with nature through meditation, bringing your awareness into the present moment. The most important way to "ground yourself" is effectively to stand barefoot on the earth. Now, most people think that we do this just for the pleasure of re-connecting to the earth, which yes, it is, but there is also another huge benefit to our energy and overall health of grounding, and that's because it acts as our **earth wire**.

Let's go back to the fact that we are all electrical beings. Now, if you think of all of your electrical items around the house, they have a plug containing a live wire which the electricity runs through. The neutral wire completes the circuit so the electricity can run. Most importantly, an earth wire that runs the electricity to the earth (aka the ground) if it overloads or if there is a fault. It is a way of expelling excess energy that will cause damage to the appliance if not dissipated. We have an earth wire for all electrical items except ourselves. Along with lacking in energy, we can also have too much energy running haywire in our system, which can cause all sorts of damage, including inflammation. Have you ever experienced static electricity where everything clings to you, and your hair stands on end? It can happen when we have too much electrical charge built up in our bodies. It is prone to occur in the winter months when we are wrapped up to shield ourselves from the elements and rarely (if ever) touch the earth directly from our skin.

I always thought that I felt so happy and content on holiday/during the summer months because I was on holiday, but there is more to it than that. It is a time when you walk on the sand, the grass or just the ground with no shoes on regularly and swim in the sea. Each day we earth/ground ourselves, removing the excess energy built up inside us with nowhere to go. We don't do that in winter. We are a generation that wears trainers with plastic soles; not only can we not earth through these, but we build electric charge from them. We need nature to ground us from a mental and physical perspective. This is where my obsessions with natural materials in the home and biophilic design stem from.

Our homes are becoming ice cream tubs; we heavily insulate ourselves. We are encasing ourselves in plastic, and one of the worst things about plastic is it can't breathe. Also, it can't absorb electrical currents and don't even get me onto it being virtually impossible to dispose of! Have you ever rubbed a balloon on your head to build the static up? Well, that's what having plastic flooring will do for you and wearing plastic shoes all the time. You can, however, ground yourselves indoors through ceramic and concrete floors if you are barefoot (another reason why those living in the Med have it made).

Connecting with the earth for 20 mins at a time allows us to reap the benefits of the natural electrical charge that it gives off and to remove the excess electrical charge that our lifestyle creates. We can also do that by swimming in the sea or lakes/rivers. Anywhere directly connected with the earth, which isn't insulated against it. Those cold water swimmers do more for their wellbeing than just cold therapy. They are regularly earthing/grounding their bodies throughout the winter months.

Grounding/earthing has been shown to stabilize our physiology at the deepest levels, reduce inflammation, pain and stress, improve blood flow, energy and sleep and generate greater wellbeing!! Well, f*ck me sideways; why aren't we all doing it every day? It's free, easy and it offers many rewards. Nature is honestly the most brilliant thing in the world; it's just a shame we humans come along and think we know better! Yes, we can use plastics and imitations of nature to create an aesthetic for longevity - but what we are losing through doing this are the natural gifts that those materials we are imitating would have offered us. Give me a floor that will weather over time because that is life. That's the beauty of life.

Nothing is eternal. At this rate, all that will be left of our lost cities will be plastic imitations of the beauty of life. How depressing, and in doing so, we have completely missed the point. Anyway, I'll get off my soapbox and back to business.

Grounding is an easy win when it comes to wellbeing, but please think twice before putting down that laminate floor or that artificial grass! It may seem like an easy win because it will last forever and require zero maintenance, but life is not about easy wins; there is always a Catch 22. If it seems too good to be true, it usually is.

14

It's perfectly normal to howl at the moon

Hear my cry!!!

Wow, I mean mid-life hits, and the proverbial sh*t hits the fan.

I thought that I was very alone in my mid-life crisis. I thought that maybe because I was a single mum, I had become so independent and taken on the male role with such fervour that I had also been gifted with a very male affliction; a mid-life crisis. But it turns out that I am not alone and that you guys are very much feeling it too! There is much to this - many valid reasons why women of our generation are experiencing this cliché of cliches.

Let me explain.

We have anxiety, worry, loss of our sense of self and the

effects of ageing (mental & physical) - but we are also in our "responsibility years." We often care for kids and potentially elderly parents whilst managing our careers, social lives (kids' social lives), the infrastructure of our homes etc. Then throw a large dose of hormonal changes from perimenopause and menopause into the mix, and you have the perfect storm.

When you look at the challenges we have thrust upon us, you can understand why we might experience a crisis followed by an awakening. We see ourselves ageing before our eyes and the finish line rapidly approaching. If at the same time, you have let your own needs get pushed to the bottom of the very deep and forever growing pile, it can easily feel like you are drowning, and no one can hear you cry. You get diagnosed with depression when really you are exhausted and need respite.

According to doctors, during perimenopause and menopause, the change in hormones, as oestrogen and progesterone levels decline, can cause many disturbances. Interfering with our sleep, causing our moods to swing and reducing our energy levels, memory loss, anxiety, weight gain, and decreased interest in things that we used to enjoy! It is no wonder that we are questioning life.

Well, that all sucks. But it's the truth, a harsh truth

but the truth nonetheless. What I have discovered is if you throw into the mix living out of alignment with your 'self', then that's when chronic illnesses and depression like to get their foot in the door.

We have so much on our spinning plates that we cannot afford to be out of alignment with who we are, as that requires far too much energy to stabilise. When we live out of alignment, we undermine ourselves making us ill. That's when we lose the essence of who we are. It's easy to bury your dreams, beliefs and values to please others, but you bury an essential part of yourself—your lifeblood.

In all of this, we have to remember that we work on a monthly cycle as women. We have hormones that change our thoughts, feelings and energy settings throughout each month for specific reasons. We are miracle workers, and our cleverly designed bodies are mind-blowing. We are built in this way so that we can create life. If you are working against your natural design, your hormonal mood swings will increase as the strain of living out of alignment causes them to get even further out of whack. The more I worked against myself, the more bi-polar I effectively became. At different stages during each month, I would be wildly optimistic and motivated. At others, I would be in an absolute slump questioning the point of life. It was all related to my hormones. Throw in the friggin moon, and you've really got my attention! How I love the synchronicities that nature sends us.

I had the copper coil fitted when I first started dating, post-marriage. It was an absolute disaster; it made me wet myself involuntarily twice. (One time was at my new boyfriend's parent's house!), so I had that removed. Then I went to natural cycles, where I monitored my monthly cycle by taking my temperature each day to know when I was ovulating etc. I had decided that I didn't want to be on any form of the contraceptive pill as they had always left me feeling flat. Oh my; the things that I learnt about my body and the signs that it gave me each cycle to let me know where I was at were amazing.

I highly recommend following a natural cycle regime and eliminating any synthesised contraception. Then your body can do what it has been built to do without interference. I will talk more about this in a later chapter, but any "fake" hormones are not good for your health and wellbeing.

Because I was spending so much time in nature, slowing down and reconnecting and grounding, my monthly cycle synced up with the moon cycle. How f*cking amazing is that? The moon is responsible for the tides through its gravitational pull. We are made up of 60% water. If you think that the moon isn't going to affect you too, you are sorely mistaken. There are so many fables and tales about lunacy (and werewolves); how can we ignore this fact? Luna is the Latin word for moon, and "lunatic" derives from the Latin word lunaticus, which originally referred to madness and diseases thought to be caused by the moon! I think they were onto something!

I am a lunatic, and I am proud of it. I am a living being, so highly connected to nature that I have synched up with it. If you allow yourself to embrace your natural state, you are too. I fought and fought against my mood swings, but now I know my cycle and the moon cycle (I track both), I have really begun to understand myself. It has allowed me to become far more accepting of who I am and that I am not always in the same state day to day, and that is normal.

I know how hard and trying midlife is. But I also know every part of ourselves is there for a reason. Sometimes we have to be more introspective than we may have previously been and recognise that we cannot just treat one thing. Hence this book.

Our bodies are effectively floating in space. If you change one thing, it will impact another and another until infinity and beyond. It's a ripple effect. You throw a stone into a lake. There is the impact, and the stone sinks, but it has set off a chain of reactions: ripples that affect life in, around and beyond the lake. The potential effects are so far-reaching. It's truly fascinating when you think about it, and it is something that can be harnessed for the greater good.

This premise is truly life-changing. You must start to recognise how powerful even the tiniest of actions have the potential to be. Making even the smallest daily changes to your lifestyle can have a massive domino effect in achieving great change. But beware, the opposite is also true with negative habits. One does not outweigh the other or receive preferential treatment. Cause and effect is a solid response, whether it starts with a positive or a negative. It's up to you to decide how you will work with that information.

I will say to you now that, as with everything else I am teaching you, you must do what is aligned with you. BUT remember that everything and everyone are interrelated, and you can't escape that.

Nature is the driver. You must learn to accept it, embrace it and move beyond the howl. Stop being the backseat driver constantly putting the brakes on and start riding alongside! Life's a journey, you need to f*cking enjoy the ride, or there is no point; you'll get to the end and say ", I didn't enjoy that" when what you really needed to do was get off of the ride that you were on and sync up with the ride that nature wanted you to go on. It knows best, and not only that, it gives you signs along the way to guide you if you just open your eyes and your mind and let yourself feel your way.

As you can imagine, I love astrology. Nuff said.

15

It's time to quit the shadow boxing

Just as there are two sides to every coin, there are two sides to each of us. Depending on which day you meet me, I'm somewhere between a librarian and a hedonist.

Beating up the version of you that doesn't conform to your standards is a complete waste of energy.

All of us have a "shadow self". It is part of who we are. Everything casts a shadow, and we are no different. We have the light and the dark inside of us. The yin and the yang. The positive and the negative (as I mentioned before).

Getting to know me again in midlife has allowed me to meet my shadow self - big time! She has played a huge part in where I am now. I know who she is, how she works and what she wants from me. She just wants to have fun at any cost. She loves a party, and she will recklessly throw away her dreams on a whim. Fighting against her has been painful and draining as she doesn't give a sh*t. Once I acknowledged and embraced her into my life without allowing her to run the show - the game changed.

You first need to recognise that you have a dark/shadow self and then embrace your darkness and integrate it within you as it is a part of you. You then have a choice of how to move forward.

This Native American parable of the Two Wolves gives you the answer:

An old Cherokee is teaching his grandson about life. "A fight is going on inside me," he said to the boy.

"It is a terrible fight, and it is between two wolves. One is evil – he is anger, envy, sorrow, regret, greed, arrogance, self-pity, guilt, resentment, inferiority, lies, false pride, superiority, and ego."

He continued, "The other is good – he is joy, peace, love, hope, serenity, humility, kindness, benevolence, empathy, generosity, truth, compassion, and faith. The same fight is going on inside you and inside every other person, too."

The grandson thought about it for a minute and then asked his grandfather, "Which wolf will win?"

The old Cherokee simply replied, "The one you feed."

I no longer feed my shadow self. She got fed waaaaay too much in my late twenties and early thirties, and when I was feeling low in my early forties, she really got her foot in the door, but now I know she is there. She won't be beaten, and she is determined and fearless. She is entertaining and wild and constantly wants to make a bid for freedom. She just makes me laugh. I love that about her - about me.

Integrating my shadow into my life took time. Time to accept that I wasn't the perfect girl that I thought I was, but none of us are perfect. There is no way we can be because we need the imperfect to remind us of what perfect is. There cannot be a state of living without its counterpart death, just as there cannot be a success without failure. The push and the pull of life, its ebb and flow, keep us striving and growing. If we didn't have our shadow selves within us, no one would strive to achieve, progress in the world and evolution would stop, and the human race would die out.

Stop berating yourself for all the parts of yourself that you dislike. They are you. We all have parts that we don't like, but the best way of dealing with them is to acknowledge that they exist and just stop feeding them. That way, they will be there on your journey with you to bring an extra pulse to your lifeblood.

They are a valid part of you, but they won't be running the show because that show is a complete shi*t show more often than not! You get to choose how you want to conduct yourself (we are all electrical conductors transmitting our energies). If you don't like the way you are currently showing up/conducting yourself, start feeding the parts that you do like but remember you don't have to be one way or another. You are the all, and when you embrace all parts, you can be whole again - an absolute necessity for living an aligned life.

EXERCISE 8 – EMBRACING YOUR SHADOW:

Part 1

Write down all of the parts of your personality that you dislike, e.g. lazy, sad, angry, bitter, impulsive, hedonistic. Anything you feel rises to the surface when you read this chapter or has popped into your head as you have read this book.

Part 2

Now, look at what may be behind those personality traits. Start acknowledging and questioning them. For example, are you really lazy or just lost focus? None of us are lazy when we are clear on our purpose. Where does the bitterness come from, and how can I absolve it? How can I use my hedonism to achieve pleasure without creating guilt?

Once you are brave enough to face up to the parts of you that you don't like and recognise them, you can start to change them for good. Your shadow is a place of teaching.

I am 100% librarian mixed with a hedonist but now I know how to use all aspects of my personality traits for the greater good.

I thought I was boring but actually I am just very thoughtful and when it comes to hedonism this has been my greatest driver towards feeling my feelings and setting myself on a path for pleasure but not at all costs. Considered pleasure that works for me. I like to think of it as happiness.

16

I couldn't be fake about anything; my facial expressions would give me away

My old boss once told me that he could tell exactly what I thought when he briefed me on a project with my facial expressions, which wasn't a good thing! I also can't help but overshare my experiences and urge to make others feel better by telling them my worst anecdotes. (My favourite is about being hit on the head by a level crossing). I also cannot help but invite anyone I speak to who seems lonely on holiday or a trip and then regret it when the words come out of my mouth.

I am beyond observant. I notice everything. I can literally smell, taste, hear and see any changes in my environment. Sometimes I think I should have been a detective, but I can't stand violence, so I guess a food taster would suit my skill set better.

As I mentioned before, when I was in my twenties, I had my ears pinned back after a lifetime of teasing. My body expelled the string used to tie them back to my great amusement. I loved showing people the string hanging out from behind my ear. It didn't occur to me to cut it off! I also managed to expel the Botox that I had in my frown lines between my eyebrows which I had done when I first got divorced, to feel better about myself. I think I had to have three rounds of it and give up green tea because it just didn't do anything to me initially.

I enjoyed the feeling of being lighter on my brow, it was a fake calm, but I didn't enjoy not being able to use my eyebrows! Did you know that we used our eyebrows to send silent signals to each other back in the old days of a hunter-gatherer? As an expressive person, this did bother me, so the Botox was a no, and the fact that it's a toxin doesn't align with my beliefs, but I completely understand why people use it. Anyway, it turns out that I am a highly sensitive person. I'm not the 'high maintenance' person people have told me I am in the past or 'overly sensitive'.

Being an HSP is my superpower. It has taught me how to live a life of alignment. Now I only use natural, paraben and chemical free skincare. I cannot tolerate the feel or, least of all, the smell of synthetics. I use oils on my face and my body. I don't buy into 'fad' beauty regimes or scientifically created products. I believe that nature is my benchmark and food is my medicine, and I aim to stay as close to this premise as I realistically can. It keeps me connected to nature and saves me a fortune on beauty products which means that my essential beauty kit is minimal. I can immediately tell if a product is fake from its smell. I'm basically like a sniffer dog.

I haven't worn 'perfume' for about ten years now. If someone walks past me wearing perfume or a strong aftershave, it literally gives me a headache, and if it's very strong, it will make me cough! I am constantly searching for alcohol free, natural based perfumes, but in all honesty, it is easier just to use essential oils because that way, I get the benefit of the oil's power at the same time as the beauty of their smell. I wear an orange essential oil which I dab behind my ears when I go out (call me crazy!), and I mix it with coconut oil as a body moisturiser. I love the smell of oranges; I find it so uplifting; it reminds me of summer and all things good. Not sure you can ask for more from life than being perfumed with something that incredible. It makes me happy.

When I go away on trips, I have been known to remove synthetic reed diffusers, badly made potpourri, and dodgy smelling candles. Or, my absolute worst, plugins and I hide them away in cupboards. I use my own lavender oil to override any bad smells for my pillowcase. It adds another dimension of excitement to my travels. It's a bit like a treasure hunt.

I have upgraded all of my cleaning products to natural ones as I realistically can. Vinegar and bicarb of soda feature heavily, along with essential oils. It is far more pleasurable to use them, the house smells nicer, and the massive win is that they aren't bad for your health! Chemical cleaning items are dangerous. Inhaling all those chemicals regularly isn't good for you, and it isn't necessary.

When it comes to what I put into my body, I have learned to stay close to nature, i.e. organic whole foods. I know that they are what my body will respond to the best. I don't always win at this, but I try to set myself up for success by having the right food in the house, preparing meals or cheating with good quality freezer-ready meals. I know this isn't ideal, but sometimes we gotta do what we gotta do. If I want a treat, I make sure that it is a high quality piece of chocolate or similar. I don't eat gluten or dairy as I am intolerant to it, which pretty much rules out any fun anyway.

I do the best I can when it comes to eating this way. I am human, and I do slip. I sometimes eat the kid's crisps and chocolate when they are in bed, but I wake up with brain fog and what feels like a hangover the next day. If I eat crap, I feel crap. It's as simple as that. Sugar kills me. I know how dull it sounds, but it's a blessing because I literally can't eat badly without paying the price. Unless I want to be bedridden, there is no point because that's how bad it gets. I know how I respond to certain foods, so I am responsible for the effects if I eat them. I can complain about low energy and brain fog, but if I am inflicting this on myself by eating crap, only I can change it. There is no miracle pill. I use a mixture of kinesiology and homoeopathy for my health needs. I also love crystals, reiki and any other energetic healings. They make complete sense to me.

When working in London in my twenties, I developed terrible acne. I went to the doctors and tried every spot cream out there. I had a spot/boil on my chin that was so painful I had to have a steroid injection. I remember going back to work with a little plaster over it. I felt like an absolute twat, but I found it somewhat amusing! Eventually, after some blood tests (which saw me passing out in the hospital where I had them and then nearly passing out again when I came round and they told me I was in the hospital), the doctor put me on Roaccutane. It cleared my spots whilst peeling off most of the skin on my face and lips. It was a painful process, but it did the job.

I went on to have quite a bad car accident in my thirties, and afterwards, my acne returned. I wasn't keen to have Roaccutane again, and I was trying to get pregnant, so I suffered with it. After reaching a dead end with the doctors, I sought alternative advice, which led me on my clean eating journey, healed me, and also completely cleared my acne without any meds!

EXERCISE 9 – NAME THAT ILL:

Now I'm going to ask you to do an exercise which you aren't going to like, but I promise it will help you. I will ask you to acknowledge all the places where you feel you aren't being truthful with yourself. I want you to list all your random ills, aches and pains, and health maintenance that bothers you but you don't do anything about. The things that weigh on your mind consciously and unconsciously.

Here are some examples; overdue dentist appointments, pain in the joint of your index finger, pain in the stomach, spots on the chin, headaches in the afternoon, brain fog, forgetfulness, tiredness, lethargy, tearfulness, bloated stomach etc.

Once you have your list, I want you to look at where you are at and how you can make some headway to solve/heal these. Eg, book your dentist appointment (this is mainly aimed at me right now!), go to the doctors, get a food intolerance test, speak to your friends and see if they have experienced similar and ask their advice.

This last one has been life-changing for me. I wrestled with a lot of chronic illnesses without ever asking for help. Since I started asking, I have learnt so much about holistic health I could write a book!

The moral of this story is that to make a change; you need to start looking at why you have symptoms that are bothering you and find out what is causing them. Don't just ignore them and 'hope' that they will disappear. They are there as a very clever red flag from your body telling you that something is amiss and that you need to address it. It is not about finding a way of stopping that symptom, e.g. Roaccutane. That is plastering over the cracks. It's like plugging a leak, but the pressure will just build up behind the plug, and it will find another way out; you need to find out where the leak is coming from. More often than not, the symptoms will all relate to stress.

Stress is effectively adverse amounts of 'pressure' on an object or person. When I was under considerable emotional strain during my marriage, the break up of my marriage and the aftermath, my digestion pretty much gave up. My body could only do so much. All it had left in it was to keep me alive. It could not deal with digesting complex, highly processed foods as that required way too much energy, which was in short supply. I had to clean my diet and drink loads of filtered water, which cured all of my ills. It's not rocket science. The more 'processed' a food item is, the more unnatural items it contains and the harder our digestion has to work to break it down and digest it. We are not evolved to deal with the processed foods and amounts of stress we put upon ourselves. We are our own worst enemy. If you are anything like I was, I buried my head in the sand until I was virtually incapacitated. It took that much to get my attention.

Spoiler alert: You are what you eat, and there isn't is a magic pill to cure all ills.

I feel like I've just told a 5-year old that Santa isn't real.

17

The myth of the miracle pill

Okay, I feel like a right b*tch rubbing it in, but there is no miracle pill to cure all ailments. I often went to the doctors wishing/hoping for a diagnosis they could treat with a magic pill. I wish there were, I'm telling you. There wasn't. There isn't.

My only option was anti-depressants which they gave me prescription after prescription for, but I never felt truly 'depressed'. I was full of hope on some days, but I found life overwhelming and hard and would cry; and I wanted it all to stop, but I didn't want to medicate away the small amounts of joy that I was feeling. They were my lifeline. I wanted to understand why I felt the way I did. On reflection, I was just going through a f*cking hard time, and it was perfectly understandable that I was ill and a bit low, and I'm a woman!

You are busy and stressed; you are trying to spin the plates and make it look easy, but it isn't. It's normal these days to be chronically ill. The bad news is that 'chronic' means incurable. The good news is that I know that that isn't true. Yes, there is no 'magic pill' to cure chronic illness, but there is the most accessible cure of all, which is in our hands, and that is our lifestyle choices. We are a generation of drug users. We take antibiotics at the drop of a hat. We just want a cure, and we don't want any fuss. If we can have a prescription, then we are happy. We will medicate till the cows come home because it's easy. We all like easy. I like easy! I fell into the drug-taking trap in a big way over the last few years. The pendulum went full swing for me. I went from prescription meds to every supplement I could get my hands on. I had been bio-hacking my health issues ever since I got clean (food wise), and I noticed that I had gone from one extreme to another.

Meds and supplements are pretty much two sides to the same coin. Yes, there is very little harm in taking supplements as they are au natural. The damage came for me from the endless shopping list of supplements I took at vast expense. I remember going on holiday for a week and bagging up all my capsules, pills, powders and vials of supplements and thinking that I would surely get arrested if security searched my suitcase. I was rattling with the number of pills and powders I was taking every day to help with my chronic illnesses, which were all due to extreme stress. All I was doing was creating so much more stress as I tried to earn enough money to pay for my supplement habit! It was insane! I didn't even know what the supplements were cut with! I felt like a drug addict, and it probably cost me about the same! I was obsessed.

Our health is something that requires balance. Supplements can help us rebalance, but self-diagnosing and bio-hacking can become extreme. They are an unhealthy obsession and can become a disorder in themselves. When given the correct environment and nutrition (like the plant analogy from earlier), our bodies rebalance themselves. They self-heal. I know because I have done it. Again, you are treating the symptom with supplements and not looking at the underlying problem.

In some cases where the damage to the body and its nervous system is extensive, support from supplements and meds can help improve a person's mental capacity to make the lifestyle changes they require to come off the meds. I am not saying that there isn't a place for these; I am just saying that we mustn't lean so heavily on them that they become an addiction. They shouldn't be the first line of defence. Everything in moderation, as my mum would say.

Finding alignment in your mind and balance in your lifestyle is the key to wellbeing and true happiness (and that's our life goal, folks)!

The one thing that I do swear by right now for supplementation is magnesium. It has been a game-changer for me. Currently, pretty much everyone is magnesium deficient. It gets used up more quickly when under stress, and we are a generation of stress heads. Magnesium can help reduce anxiety, strengthen bones, reduce fatigue, aid restful sleep and improve symptoms of restless legs. I take two tablets every night before bed to help me sleep, stop my restless legs and reduce anxiety. I also bathe in magnesium salts, and I really notice the difference. The purist in me would say that I 'should' be getting more of this by eating a higher magnesium diet. Whilst I'm still building the best infrastructure of my life, I will incorporate this life hack. Then I'll have the energy and motivation to make the appropriate changes not to require them in the future. I don't like being beholden to something outside of myself for my health and wellbeing. That seems too unnerving for me knowing how easy it is to lose everything.

EXERCISE 10 – NAME THAT PILL:

Okay, I want you to write down a list of all the supplements you are taking and any meds, what they are for and their regularity. Then I want you to write down the monthly cost. Then I want you to think about what you could use this money for instead that would improve your happiness levels.

E.g. If I had £50 a month extra, I would spend it on a monthly massage.

Then think about how you could reduce the monthly spend on your supplements to realise this massage. Could you introduce a new food group to your diet each day that contains that supplement in its natural form at a fraction of the price?

Do what you need to do when it comes to finding a supplement or meds that will give you the strength to help you through a rough patch and make the step changes to improve your health and wellbeing. However, don't become reliant on them. It's so easy to get hooked on life hacks. I well know! Think of them as a crutch that you are using whilst you get all the cogs in the right place to restart the machine that is your body. Then it will function smoothly and effectively and work for you. They are not a long-term solution. You are the long-term solution, and focussing on your happiness will improve your health no end! So book the massage and ditch the powders and pills (they are all pretty much placebo anyway)!

18

Stay away from bad vibes

There are a lot of bad vibes out there coming your way. There's negative energy that's gonna f*ck up your circuit so much that you cannot conduct your energy positively. When you allow yourself the luxury of becoming aware of what is going on around you and how it makes you feel, you realise the extent of the negativity currently impacting your life. Without you even realising it, this is a major win on the happiness scales as you can choose to simply cut these circuit breakers out of your life.

Cutting out the mainstream media/news is the simplest route to peace. Stop listening to it and consuming it. Have you noticed most things that get reported are bad news? Stuff that you wouldn't know if no mainstream media shared the stories. What you don't know doesn't hurt you. I know that sounds naïve, but I wouldn't know these things without media. I wouldn't know that a teenager just murdered a granny or a policeman raped a woman. Bad things happen. I know that; I'm aware of it. I don't need constant reminders.

I don't want my girls to hear about all the brutalities of life in one hit. They will learn in time through life experience. I didn't grow up listening to the horrors of life reported every hour of each day. I turn the radio off when the news comes on. I mean, movies and TV programs have suggested viewer age ratings and a watershed after which they can swear. Still, on the news, we hear about rape, murder and all sorts of horrors at the drop of a hat! How f*cking depressing and frightening is that. I don't want to explain what 'rape' means to my eight-year-old.

It is also a self-fulfilling prophecy. If the news reports a recession about to hit, then a recession will hit as everyone changes their spending habits and fears a recession. Fait acompli. If they hadn't reported it, it probably wouldn't have happened, and that's not me being a conspiracy theorist; that's just pointing out the obvious. It's the same with anything. If they report food shortages, everyone panic buys. Of course, they will. They trust the media, and the scarcity appears whether they are real or not.

So I stay away from the mainstream news channels. I keep up with the narrative on things I am interested in knowing about, but I do my own research. I have had to be selfish and focus on my rise. War is an alien concept to me as an HSP. How does killing help anyone? Surely, we are more sophisticated than that. Imagine if we were all to work to help each other? Imagine if happiness was, in fact, everyone's overall goal? We wouldn't have to worry about being power hungry or controlling others through manipulation or financial coercion. We would all be slotted into our own place in the world and make it better using our own unique talents and gifts.

It takes me on to social media. It is a different concept from mainstream media. The content doesn't appear to be so heavily censored, and individuals create it by sharing their gifts, skills, art and stories! It can be a huge inspiration and provide massive support and community. My writing career began on Instagram as I started to share my search for happiness. I amassed a kind, loving, inspiring and caring following who were and continue to be a great support, like my own cheerleading group. They pick me up when I am down, congratulating me on my wins. I am beyond grateful because I don't know where I would have been without them. Gina Ford had not written a book about life post-divorce as a mid-life mum, so I was clueless! I felt very, very alone when I first left my marriage.

Initially, I got all the good stuff out of socials, but then I started the comparison game, a few people made bitchy comments and overwhelm kicked in. I took myself out of the ring for a while as the negative outweighed the positive. I am learning to manage it much better. It's not easy, though and needs to be taken with a pinch of salt.

If I'm honest, I would rather it didn't exist in a way as it is yet another thing to add to our spinning plates. However, it also offers me an amazing platform to share my story and provide hope, advice and inspiration for others. It's a bit of a toxic relationship. I often write a list of negatives v's positives to allow myself to get my head around whether it needs to continue to exist in my life. Then I remind myself of why I am there, and that is to share my experiences so that others (aka you guys) can benefit from what I have learnt. It isn't about the comments, likes and followers; it is about how I can help, but sometimes I can't help getting caught up in the popularity contest. We are all human.

This thought takes me on to people in general. I like to think of myself as a good person. I genuinely want the best for others (hence writing this book). I have learnt from many painful experiences that not everyone feels the same. I am programmed to see the best in people and assume that everyone is honest and kind. I was naïve, and they aren't. They continue to surprise me!! Some people, it seems, can be f*cking horrible! I have experienced toxic relationships on a romantic level, a work level and a friendship/acquaintance level. I have wrestled heavily with their impact on my mental health. I tried to make myself stronger to cope with some of them but soon realised that I was fighting a losing battle. If someone is constantly trying to tear you down or shows no empathy for you, then cut ties with them if you can or keep your distance and protect your energy.

There are drains and radiators out there. Stick with the radiators. What people say to you and how they treat you can and does have a massive impact on your mental health. Words are like spells. If they are kind, positive and encouraging words, they can work to great effect. If they are negative, harsh and brutal, they can be a curse. Do not underestimate this. It is not you being overly sensitive or a bit pathetic. It is you being a kind and compassionate human being. I have learnt/am still learning to steel myself to any negativity directed at me. I've experienced a considerable amount of it and continue to as I rebuild my life. I have learnt that it's not about me. It's about how I trigger a person's insecurities. I have had relationships where the 'better' I was, the more my partner despised me. That was hard and harsh and upsetting and a completely non-win situation. In that instance, you need to be grateful that you can walk away. And walk away you must because being with someone constantly trying to blow out your light means that they will eventually succeed.

EXERCISE 11 – CUTTING DOWN THE CHRISTMAS CARD LIST:

Part 1

I want you to think about the negative people or influences in your life, write them down and then burn that piece of paper with a huge ceremony. You must then decide how much access they are allowed to you and your precious energy.

Part 2

I also want you to do a social media mental health audit. Write down a list of all the positives that it offers you and a list of all the negatives. (If you don't need it in your life, get rid and welcome in freedom). If you do need it for your work, community support etc., then look at what boundaries you can put in place to limit the negativity. i.e. I limit how much time I spend on it. I try not to scroll or go down rabbit holes as they not only throw me into the comparison game. I'm generally not winning in my head, but they also waste my time!!! We don't have time to waste.

Part 3

Open your awareness to the negativity of the mainstream news. Become curious about how one-sided it is and how this could affect you. Be brave enough to realise that not knowing everything about world politics isn't something to be ashamed of if it is detrimental to your mental health and overall wellbeing. If it is scaring you, walk away.

What we get out of life is ultimately our responsibility. We can't blame others, the government, our neighbour's dog who barked at us the other day or the person who cut in front of us while driving and created a rage.

When we live in true congruence, there isn't much that can destroy our peace as it comes from the inside, but it takes some work/effort to reach that level of emancipation. I'm not saying you will be happy 100% of the time, as that's not realistic. But you will be strong, resilient and certain enough in yourself that the bad vibes thrown at you will bounce back off again. That's the goal. To learn how to cope with grace and vigour and, best of all, some good humour (my favourite meme is "I've met some pricks in my time, but you, my friend, are the f*cking cactus").

I want you to get to a place where you know that no matter what life throws at you, you have the tools which equip you to deal with it and that you have a support system (your own little solar system, let's say) that is there with you to keep your light shining even when it feels dark.

19

Finding faith whether you choose to believe in a God or not

When you are boxed in so tight with dead ends all around you, at some point, you must decide to take a risk on yourself and your dreams. Nothing good comes without taking a risk but taking a chance on yourself is the hardest thing when it puts your entire infrastructure at risk.

Taking a risk on myself whilst flying solo with two dependants and having the ultimate responsibility for them has been the f*cking hardest thing in the world. Trusting that I have the answers and know which way to steer my ship has been testing. Finding trust in myself, aka faith, has been the answer.

Finding faith in yourself is necessary for any healing to have an impact. Affirmations and positive thinking can only work when you can actually relate to them for yourself when you understand who you are. If you don't permit yourself to embody who you really are, nothing works, and I speak from experience.

Finding faith has been a big journey, with many hard lessons. I come from a religious family, and the teachings of the Bible are almost second-nature, but I couldn't get to grips with the conformity of organised religion and the way it was taught. It just didn't resonate with me. But finding a "faith" seemed to be my missing link.

At so many points after I got divorced, I had experiences that were so incredible that they reinforced my faith in something (I didn't know what). One day I was out for a walk with a friend, and we were talking about life and goals and out of nowhere, I said that I would love to write for the Sunday Times Style Magazine. It sounded like a crazy idea as I hadn't written for anyone at the time other than doing some copywriting jobs. When I told my friends my plan, there was a LOT of negative feedback…

Who was I to write for them? What did I have to offer? Writers worked for years to get that opportunity - why should I be any different?

It makes me laugh even thinking about it. A couple of weeks later, after many random events took place, I was on the phone with a journalist. She was writing an article for a magazine and wanted to ask me some questions about dating in my 40s. She interviewed me whilst my girls ran around my legs, trying to get my attention. At the end of the call, I asked her which magazine she was writing for, and she told me it was the ST Style Magazine. My dream was coming true! I literally couldn't believe it, so I asked if I could be name-checked or write something additional, but the answer was a resounding no. She told me she would send over the article for me to see before it ran, but I never heard back from her again. I was pretty disappointed, but I took heart from the fact that I got so close!

I must have mentioned this happening on my IG and tagged the ST Style Magazine as I shared my journey. The next thing I knew, I had an email from one of the editors commissioning me to write an article about dating in my 40s!! WTAF!! I cannot tell you how that made me feel. I was walking on air. I was writing for them, but I was also getting paid for it!! It was unbelievable. Like my friends had said, most people work for years to get this kind of opportunity, and there it was for me, like a shiny, golden gift to reinforce my faith in life.

I loved writing the article. I was so proud of myself. I got it filed in plenty of time and paid for my work. I was apprehensive about it running, bearing in mind my topic, and it was a pretty open and vulnerable piece. Still, I wrote it to help other women in the same position, which gave me a sense of fulfilment. I dared to dream about how this would change my life and get me further toward my goals, and life was good. I didn't anticipate what would happen next. The day before my article was due to run, Covid entered our lives, and the magazine pulled my piece as we all went into lockdown. By the time we came out of lockdown and life as we knew it returned, my article was completely outdated as the dating arena had completely changed.

I was heartbroken. I cannot deny how much that hurt me. I was so, so close, teetering on the edge of glory and then it was all ripped away. Thank goodness the lockdown summer was so nice, and I could stay home and lick my wounds whilst I rallied myself and questioned my faith.

The article I wrote eluded a similar scenario that I had had in my first foray into dating after divorce.

I remember thinking that I would find my prince charming now I had left my marriage. It started with a trip to Antigua that I was fortunate enough for my parents to pay for me to join them and my sisters (and their kids) as my 40th birthday present. I travelled alone, and I daydreamed about my prince on the flight. He would be European, not British. I was fed up with the uncouth British men, he would be handsome, self-assured, successful, and a bit like James Bond, and we would live happily ever after. He would be the answer to my prayers. I would never have to worry about anything again (a bit like a rug that I once bought for the house that I thought would bring me the happiness I desperately sought!).

So the holiday came and went, and nothing out of the ordinary took place. I remember my younger sister trying to sell me off to some dodgy guy at the bar in the marina, but he wasn't overly interested! Jeez! On the last day, I decided to walk down the beach a bit further on my own to where it was pretty much deserted. I was sunburnt, wind-swept and covered in sand and salt (my ideal). I lay down and read a book and let the escapism of the story carry me away. Then I noticed someone pull up to the beach in a little grey rib (a boat you use to get around in when you have a yacht) about five metres away from me.

I tried to focus on my book, but I was intrigued to see a guy jump out with a bag and take out a load of bits. Okay, I couldn't help but watch him over my book, and he clearly knew what he was doing. The sun was so bright that I couldn't get a good look at him, but he looked pretty fit (if you know what I mean) and definitely not a teenager, so that was a start. It's not so much fun if you are old enough to be their mum! He deftly put together a windsurf and then headed out on it into the beautiful turquoise Caribbean sea.

After not very long, he was back on the beach and packing away his kit. It was not an easy task, like putting away a pop-up tent that you have for the kids. He was making it look easier than I would have tbh. At the same time, a voice in my head was saying to me very, very loudly 'say something to him.' My heart was beating louder and louder as the voice in my head became louder and louder. I was trying to fight back. It was telling me not to waste this opportunity. To say hi. There was no one else around, and he didn't look like a mass murderer and be brave and make contact. OMG, I had a massive internal wrestle with myself. I knew I would kick myself if I didn't say hello, but I felt like a mess, and I didn't want to bother him.

Thank f*ck he spoke to me. I looked up enough times to show that I was aware that he was there, and he spoke! Praise the lord! He had saved me from me. It turned out that he was European and had just done a yacht race. He left his yacht in the harbour and had flown back over to collect it to be shipped back to

Mallorca. (You know, just your average guy). He was very handsome! He sat next to me in the sand, and we chatted. He asked why I was sitting alone, and I told him that I had just left my marriage and was getting some much-needed respite from my life and the mess I had left at home. He told me that his wife and kids were coming to meet him in two days.

Fucccccckkkkkkkkkkkkkkkkkkkkkkkkk!

Why? Why? Why?

Okay, so he was married. Not an ideal scenario, but he seemed a nice guy. He suggested we go for a drink. When he realised he didn't have any cash on him, he invited me to meet him that evening on his yacht moored in the harbour that was a stone's throw from where we were staying. He drew me a map in the sand of its location, and then he disappeared almost as quickly as he had arrived.

The dilemma ran through my mind. Do I meet him? Or do I walk away and be grateful that a man had asked me out for a drink for the first time in ten years? Instead, I decided to drag my sister and her husband along for moral support. I had a few rum punch sundowners for courage, and then off we went to find his yacht. When we arrived, he was on the phone with his family. He was very open about that. We stayed and had a few drinks as he showed us around his yacht, and then my sister and her hubby left. It was just us two under the stars on a yacht in the Antiguan harbour, wearing shorts and t-shirts as it was so warm and chatting about life. He told me about his father dying in his late forties of prostate cancer, not much older than he was now (he was 45 when I met him, I was a very tender 39). His father had ignored all of the symptoms, and he shared how angry he was at him.

I told him my sad story, and we both reflected on life. We seemed to be able to talk about everything. It was a very bittersweet time. The setting couldn't have been more perfect. He couldn't have been more perfect, apart from his wife and kids, who weren't much older than mine. He told me that he would marry me if he could live another life. I reminded him of his mum (what a line) and that if he could find me on a deserted beach in Antigua, the right person would find me. I'm not a very soppy or romantic person, but he was totally authentic and genuine with me. I believed what he said. Many of you will be scoffing at this now, but I'm not finished yet.

At around 3 am, he gave me a backie on his Brompton bike back to my villa that I was staying in with my sister. For that moment in time, life was blissful. I was riding on the back of a bike with a man I felt myself totally with. The breeze was warm, the stars were bright, the crickets were calling, and the waves were lapping. It felt like complete freedom. I will never forget that night and the feeling it created in me. It woke something up inside me that I couldn't put back to bed again. It ignited my spirit. The spirit that life had doused so many times that I didn't even think it existed anymore.

It gave me faith. Faith that even though he wasn't the person for me and never would be that the right person would find me. I was alive. And there was still hope.

We kept in touch. I even visited him once in Mallorca, it was an absolute shit show, but I'll save that story for another day. The only thing I'll say about it is that he seemed different, smaller somehow and less engaged when I saw him again, which made sense in the end. He would send me pictures of his adventures and his children. We would chat regularly, but nothing more than that. He became a good friend (although, of course, I wanted more). One day he sent me an email telling me that he had been to the doctor, and they had diagnosed him with pancreatic cancer. The prognosis wasn't good, and he could no longer be in touch with me as he would have to hand over his business and his life to his wife.

I felt physically sick. He called me 5 mins later, and

when I answered the phone, I spoke to a man who had accepted his fate. He told me that the chance of him surviving was so slim as the cancer was so advanced. He had ignored all the symptoms just like his dad. He had stepped away from his business. He would spend the rest of his days with his kids, who were 4 and 6 at the time. I didn't want him to give up. I tried to find every reason why he could live. He lived in a mountainous country where the air was clear, and his wife was a doctor. He was only 45, and he was fit and healthy. He had buckets of money to pay for treatment. He had every hope. He told me to live a good life, to love my kids and that he was happy no matter what. He had had a good life, and that was enough for him. I asked him if he could let me know how he was doing and let me know if he had lived or died. I couldn't bear not knowing. He said he would try, and we said goodbye, and I never heard from him again. My friends told me it was bullsh*t and that he had made it up to shake me off.

About nine months later, I was in my kitchen listening to some music on the radio, and a song came on that made the hairs on my arms stand on end. It was a haunting song called The Lonely Shepherd by Gheorghe Zamfir that we had listened to on the yacht in Antigua. I googled his name. He was very well known and respected in his home country, and the first thing that came up in my search was his eulogy. He had died a week previously.

I can't listen to that song again without crying; I can't write this without crying. It was a monumental and pivotal moment in my life. He had told me that he had died. And not only that, he had demonstrated to me that even the best of us dies. He had made me realise that happiness is found in every moment, no matter what is ahead and that a well-lived life is enough. He had shown me grace. He had given me faith. A faith that I couldn't previously comprehend.

I don't know about you, but this is something that I have seriously questioned in more recent years.

I couldn't understand organised religion or why it worked, but I could understand what he had shown me that the only place you can find god is within you. Heaven is a place on earth (as Belinda Carlisle well knew). When we trust in our inner knowing, we find peace, and that's when we can transcend to the eternal light. Jesus made water into wine which he gladly shared. We all have that capacity within us when we trust in ourselves. On the flip side, Rumpelstiltskin spun straw into gold in return for the queen's born and because her values were screwed, she lost her daughter.

I have had so many reality check moments from life

on my journey that I have ignored. I had a pretty bad car accident in my early 30s. I got hit by a foreign lorry when I was going 70mph on the M25 in rush hour. I watched it pull across and get stuck on the side of my Mini. As it pulled away, I started screaming, my car started to spin, and my airbags went off and hit me, one from the side and one from the front, and each time I thought I was dead. I thought it was the impact of other cars, and my time was up.

By some miracle, I went back down the M25 with traffic driving toward me. I had to steer myself onto the hard shoulder at high speed; my absolute worst skill is reversing. It even crossed my mind how typical this was that I would have to reverse my way out of this situation! Once I got myself to a standstill after steering myself into the side reservation, I crawled over to my passenger door to climb out as the driver's door was wedged shut. Then I ran away from it and got into the crash position on the roadside (as clearly I have watched too many films). I had no idea that when your airbags go off, they fill the car with particles which look like smoke. I thought that the car was on fire and about to explode. It wasn't.

A couple picked me up off the floor. I think they were more shaken than I was at the time.

They said that they had watched the whole thing

unfold in front of them and that they couldn't believe that I was still alive. The lady was almost hysterical. They called my boyfriend (who would then go on to be my husband) to come and pick me up when I refused an ambulance. I thought I was fine. I felt guilty about creating a standstill on the M25 on a Friday night during rush hour!

How little I cared for myself, my default mode was guilt. I was also concerned about whether I had got my new white jeans dirty!

I wasn't fine. But I didn't have a scratch on me. I had no concept of how much that experience would scar me mentally. I didn't realise until a long time after that I had PTSD. I never spoke to anyone about those thoughts apart from a therapist a while later. I found it hard to drive on roads with more than one lane, which was slightly problematic. I worried, and the main thing I didn't want was to become isolated and unable to get around (I later healed this paranoia through acupuncture, just FYI)! I cried every time I heard a siren or saw an accident and constantly questioned why I had been spared when others weren't.

I mean, WTAF, I just carried on as normal. There was no physical harm, so there was no point making a big deal of it was my mentality (and many of us share the same mindset when it comes to mental health). I mean christ almighty! My mind thought that I was surely dead when the lorry first hit, let alone when each airbag went off, which I mistakenly took as cars hitting me. In my head, I was dead.

It opened a pandora's box in my head that I had never considered before - I was actually going to die one day.

Have you ever stopped to question your mortality? I can't believe that I got as far as I did without even considering it. My kids are much more aware. I think that the Universe was constantly giving me nudges to wake up to life. Take the very lucky escape that I had from the Boxing Day tsunami in Thailand. On the day of the tsunami, I had just flown into Phuket in Thailand to get the ferry over to Koh Phi Phi for a well-earned holiday. I was blissfully ignorant of the catastrophe unfolding around me as I made several decisions that were really unlike me but ultimately saved my life. We got into a taxi to go to the beach whilst waiting for our ferry. However, I stopped the taxi as we went past a hotel with a pool and suggested we go there and sit by the pool for an hour instead (that's the sun worshipper in me). If I hadn't followed my intuition, I would have been sunbathing by the water's edge or swimming in the sea when the wave hit. That spontaneous decision probably saved our lives as the beach in Patong was annihilated.

It was a real sliding doors moment between life and death. It shook me up, but it didn't wake me up. It must have been terrifying for my family to watch it on TV. I remember my mum calling me. When I answered the phone, she was hysterical. I didn't know wtf was going on. We hadn't even witnessed any of it as we were in a marina that was sheltered from the wave. My family continued to try and call me, but the calls kept cutting off as the chaos ensued, and no one in Phuket knew what was going on. It was like Chinese whispers, and we didn't know what to believe. We spent that night sleeping on the floor in a hotel that had taken in displaced people. We managed to fly out the next day. Our flight was eerily empty apart from a couple of injured passengers. When we got to Singapore and watched the completely uncensored news, I had to switch off to the devastation that had reigned around me whilst I walked away unscathed.

My parents told me it was because they had prayed for me. I just went along with them at the time, but now I believe them and understand the importance of unwavering faith. Whether you believe in organised religion or not, you can't underestimate the power of prayer. For the spiritually awakened, prayer is in the form of affirmations and gratitude, but it is still prayer. Group prayer has even stronger results, hence the necessity for churches and everyone in a space to focus on the same thing at once. Logically, this creates energy, and I have witnessed what the mind can manifest. There has been a home, an amazing work opportunity, a man (although he died, which isn't a great start) and numerous other inconceivable things. Words and thoughts are like spells. They have a vibration, and they are how we create everything around us. Everything was once an idea. It's only when we start acting on our thoughts that they become a reality. Things don't just happen by magic. You are here to create the magic.

Randomly, on a happier note, I also won two tickets to Iceland with less danger involved after obsessing over wanting to go! It's crazy but true! That's why you should be careful of what you wish for. If you constantly worry about something happening, it will find you. It's a self-fulfilling prophecy, but as I said, the flip side is true, too, and that's where the magic lies. Believing you can achieve the dreams lodged in your mind is key to your happiness, but this system works hand in hand with gratitude for the here and now. To be truly happy in the future, you need to learn to be truly happy in the now with what you have and have faith that everything is working out exactly as it is meant to.

This isn't always easy, I know. When things are really bad, and your life has crumbled, toxic positivity can be damaging and delusional.

Sometimes we feel like we have to put on a brave face when life sucks. This isn't true. Learning to accept a situation and feel our way through it is essential. Once we feel all the feels, we can let the pain pass, but if we ignore it and "pretend" we are happy, we start chipping away at our sense of self. Gratitude for those moments and dealing with them allows us to find peace and begin simmering our happiness levels.

I went through my marriage being toxically positive. Always putting a smile and a brave face on when inside, I felt like I was dying. All I did was dig a deeper hole for everyone involved. Walking away was the hardest thing I have ever had to do, but I did it to save us - all of us: my ex-husband, me and most of all, our children. Damage limitation. If I had stayed pretending that everything was okay, the poison would have gotten stronger and tasted viler.

EXERCISE 12 – FIRMING UP YOUR BELIEF SYSTEM:

Okay, I want you to spend a moment thinking and writing about your current belief system and how it's working for you. What are your beliefs when it comes to faith? Do you have faith in yourself, or do you look for external validations of your beliefs? When something goes wrong, do you feel anchored in yourself, or does everything around you crumble? Do you believe in yourself?

Next, I want you to think of something to look out for. Anything, it may be a butterfly, a JCB, a red heart, a chipmunk or a purple car. I want you to focus on it, and I want you to keep your eyes open for it.

Don't change your day, but be super aware of what you are looking for because it will find you. It may not be where you expected to see it. It may be on a book cover that you glance at, a tv program that you are watching with the kids, or knitted into the cardigan that the lady you pass on the street is wearing. But I promise you will see it if you focus your sights on it. You must use this as a reminder that what you think aligns with what is and that you are in charge. Don't question or rationalise your thoughts. Just have faith!

Finding faith in yourself is the epiphany that you are looking for. You are the creator. You are the way, the truth and the life. The Bible is full of wisdom if you start looking at interpreting it from a slightly different perspective. It was translated from a different language in ancient times. The lessons make so much sense, but they imply that we are looking outside ourselves. Look what happens when you type a sentence in a translator online app to translate it to a different language. When you use it on a local…quite often, you can be completely off the mark! It is all inside you, and perhaps that's what it's meant to say, but the translation went awry.

We all see and experience things differently. Have you ever considered that there is nothing that we have ever experienced outside of our senses? Outside of our sight, smell, taste, hearing and touch? They are our only inputs. We then process these to create our reality. You've got to find faith in yourself and how you interpret your inputs before finding true happiness.

The devil is your shadow self, it's always there tempting you, and if you choose to feed the shadow, you will be in your own personal hell. You cannot find happiness in a man, a rug or a million holidays. You find happiness when you feed your higher self and laugh in the face of the devil; he's always so much fun but best kept at arm's length.

I learnt from harsh experiences that no one was coming to save me, so I had to decide to do it for myself. I literally woke up and smelt the coffee. I took myself through the exercises in this book. I wrote out a plan of how I wanted myself and my life to look, where my values lay and what my beliefs were. I started to live very intentionally by them, not allowing the excuses to hold me back. I made (and continue to make) aligned choices toward my dreams. I did not allow the setbacks or negativity to derail me.

I battled chronic fatigue, two little girls to nurture (and the lion's share of the care) and very little money or financial support. I stole a pack of school socks for my daughter from Sainsbury's at my lowest. I had a very tricky relationship with my ex-husband on top. There were very few supporters, and my home, career, friendship group and life to rebuild. Also, failed attempts at finding a new partner (which were pretty painful but are another book in itself)—and not forgetting to mention a complete lack of faith in myself.

It wasn't easy, to say the least. My family despaired of me. My friends weren't anywhere to be seen (apart from a few beauties I will value to the day I die). It took time, patience, determination, saying goodbye to old habits (qualities that I had previously lacked) and a few false starts to get the wheels in motion. Things started to fall into place like magic once I did, and life started to make sense again. Waking up in the morning was no longer filled with angst, worry and impending doom that I had to breathe through to function. Happiness began to seep back into my being. Now I have so much faith in myself that I have written this book so that you can find yourself and your faith too.

Faith in yourself will be your salvation. Learning to dance with the devil will be where you find your freedom.

N.B. I work as a Conscious Lifestylist (somewhere between a life coach, health coach, personal stylist, interior designer, cheerleader and intuitive). If you want to regain your sense of self and find more purpose and fulfilment but don't know where to start, I will help you 'style your best life' and take you from surviving to thriving at a holistic level. You can find me at **www.theconsciouslifestylist.co.uk** or on the beach.

20

It's alright for her

Oh, it's alright for her, I hear your mind say when reading this book.

It's alright for her because she is so much younger than me.

It's alright for her as she is so much slimmer than me.

It's alright for her as she has much more money than me.

It's alright for her as she has so much more time than me.

It's alright for her; she as has much more support than me.

It's alright for her because she is so much more privileged than me.

It's alright for her because her kids are older than mine.

And so on.

It's so easy to find excuses for why we cannot make changes to our lives, and I'm telling you, I get that. I get it 100%, but as I said in the previous chapter, I had a lot of challenges to get through, a lot of hurdles to overcome and a lot of constraints to work around, but

I did it. It wasn't easy, but it was worth it.

Making changes to our lives requires discomfort. No one likes discomfort and "getting out of the comfort zone", just as no one looks forward to that first day back at the gym, but once you get past that first step, you feel great!

First and foremost. You are not too old, and it is not too late. This was one of my favourite excuses not to do anything.

"I'm 40 now. It's too late for me to start a new and fulfilling career. I'll just have to make do with what I have been doing forever, which I hate and saps my energy and destroys my soul, but I'll do it anyway because what other choice do I have? I'm so old…I'm virtually at retirement age. There's no point changing now."

Society teaches us this narrative on the stereotypical life timeline. You are born, go to school, go to college/uni or straight into the workplace, find a job, get married, have kids, juggle all the balls and spin all the plates whilst saving for retirement; you retire, you die. Fun.

When I got divorced on the cusp of turning 40, I dropped off the standard timeline. I felt like I had dropped off a cliff, and I had no idea how to fly. I was bouncing off the rocks as I continued to fall. I wouldn't massively recommend this technique as it's pretty painful. I created the exercises that I have set in this book to stop you from getting so beaten up on your way to change. However, I needed the battle scars to create the change as I was clinging so tightly to the safety of my comfort zone.

Living is a privilege. Ageing is the biggest privilege out there. I watched my Auntie work and work and work and stress and stress and stress about money and saving for her retirement. She was an amazing woman, but she never followed her dreams. She was an accountant, but she couldn't have been further from that stereotype. She was a fantastic golfer, an incredible tennis player and fiercely competitive. She was fun and funny and kind and loving, but she lived in fear of mostly everything, and crazy stuff seemed to happen to her. Once a paintball flew through the passenger window of her car as she was driving. It burst on the window next to her. Because it was red, she thought she had been shot!

On another occasion, a salmon sandwich flew through her open sunroof and landed on her as she was driving. She attracted ridiculous happenings (although I can't talk as I got hit by a level crossing). She was also, mostly always, convinced that she was dying. She suffered from chronic fatigue and hypersensitivity. She would call ambulances to her aid on many occasions.

The most memorable was at Disney in Florida (her favourite place). That was an expensive one!

She visited her brother (my dad) in Canada one time. It's an epic trip to get there as he lives about a 4-hour drive north of Vancouver, and when she got there, she decided it was too dark for her, so she flew straight back home again after about two nights. She made us laugh with her eccentricities. But she had the last laugh. Her continuing health complaints and trips to the hospital finally rewarded her with an Ovarian Cancer Diagnosis just as she retired. It was advanced, and she had secondary tumours. She fought it with all her might, but she didn't win against this opponent.

Her last breath became my first breath of living again. Without her death, I would not have found the courage to live and believe in myself truly. I refused to let her death be in vain. I am also frighteningly similar in disposition to her. She was no longer living, so the best thing I could do to honour her was embrace life and every aspect of who I am. Watching the course of her later life, I knew that I needed to start making better choices for myself. She never married, and she never had a family of her own. She never really stepped into the person that she could be. She was never really her true self. She didn't allow herself that luxury.

It's time to take radical responsibility for your life

and the aspects you can control. We can all have excuses. My kids are full of them. We learn them at a young age! But we have the power to overrule them. Seeing others lose their lives and no longer have the opportunities that I do has been a major driver for me. On the one hand, I feel like I'm running out of time. But, on the other it makes their lives feel so wasted if I don't take responsibility for my own and really make an effort to live it fully.

You have a gift of life. It's a gift that we take for granted until it's taken away - and then it's too late.

Death is a certainty. You gotta take that on board right now. One day you will no longer be on this earth. You will have had your time. Make it count!

We are programmed to be as risk averse as possible but just being alive is inherently risky. You need to decide how you want to conduct yourself. Do you want to live, or do you want to exist? Do you want to take this opportunity that you have to throw yourself into trying to get the best out of life, or are you going to squander it?

I see pain and loss and desperation and struggle all around me. I have experienced all of those things and have wanted to quit on many occasions. Yes, I am privileged. I have grown up in a beautiful and affluent part of the world. My life looks pretty nice from the outside. I have potential. I will make the most of that out of respect for those that don't get to.

You have the potential inside of you that needs to be realised in this lifetime. It is your duty as a human being to f*cking try. We can all come up with a million excuses of why we can't change our lives, and woe is me, but in reality, they are all bullsh*t. Find the motivation to be better, don't wait for a serious health scare to gee you up.

LET ME GEE YOU UP!

You are not getting out of here alive. None of us are. Make the f*cking best of what you have. Stop moaning about sh*t and saying it's alright for her because of x, y, and z. Yes, it's alright for her because she's pulled her finger out of her backside, taken on board some harsh reality checks, and done something about it.

Are you going to read this book and face up to yourself and the crap side of you that's lazy and wants to stay in the comfort zone and just see life as a 'fait accompli'? Or are you going to bloody well do something about it?

Because unless you are dead, there isn't anything stopping you, and if you are reading this book, I presume you are still breathing, which means that there is hope. You are still alive, my friend. You are one of the lucky ones, and you have one job to do today, and that is to be happy with your lot, and if that involves making a major overhaul to your life, then that is what you must do. Please don't wait until it's too late.

BECAUSE BY THEN, IT WILL BE TOO F*CKING LATE!

EXERCISE 13 – WHAT'S YOUR EXCUSE?

Simply write down all the reasons that pop into your head why none of this can work for you, i.e. I'm too busy, I'm too old, I'm too tired, I'm too fat, I'm too hard done by.

Then I want you to find a way around, over or through that hurdle because if you want something enough, you will make it happen.

As with the 'accept it; change it; or leave it' exercise earlier, you aren't ever allowed to moan about these things again unless you have f*cking tried to overcome them!!!! People are competing in the Paralympics who have no arms. If they can find a way, then so can f*cking you! Stop being a pussy and get your act together!

21

Style your Best F*cking Life

"Every choice I make makes me."

Read that. Then reread it. Then keep reading it again and again, every day, over and over until it sinks in.

You are the one who is creating your life by the big and oh so little choices that you make day after day, week after week, year after year. Funnily enough, it is often the oh so little choices that mount up to the most. Life slips by in the blink of an eye, and unless we are watchful, we can miss it. Cause and effect. Chaos and order. Life and death. It's entirely your choice.

After reading this book, I hope you realise that you are in the driving seat of your life. A terrifying thought but ultimately the route to freedom from the shackles in which you bind yourself.

Henry Ford once famously said, **"Whether you think you can, or you think you can't – you're right."**

It's non-sensical but makes complete sense.

On a similar note, the other day, my dad said to me, "everything in the universe is either a duck, or it isn't". Sometimes you have to wonder, but I have grown up with this kind of madness, so I fully embrace it! I love it! I love how wondrous life is, but I didn't always feel that way. The period where I lost myself was the most frightening years of my life. It's a paradox at every turn, a game that we are all playing and the only person we are playing against is ourselves.

It's taken me over forty years of learning, trying, failing, quitting, resting, questioning, recovering, resetting, crying, raging and starting again. This got me to the point where I know that life is not as tricky as we are led to believe it is or indeed as unrewarding and painful. It is incredibly straightforward. Do what lights you up, live by your values, enjoy the fruits of your labour, help others, be kind, give back, have faith, tread lightly, trust your intuition and go with love.

It's time my love for the big life appraisal. No one wants this, but the paradox is that you desperately need it (before life throws you a massive whammy to wake you up). You'll only realise how much you needed it after embracing it in all its mess and mayhem. To make something better, it often needs to get worse first.

EXERCISE 14:

So for this final exercise, I want you to do the following: I want YOU to man the f*ck up. I want YOU to be braver than you ever have been.I want YOU to admit to where you can improve your life. I want YOU to address where YOU are holding yourself back. And most of all, I want YOU to take action and start backing yourself and styling a f*cking brilliant life that will allow your light to burn so bright that you guide others back to themselves too.

The world is your playground; life is your oyster, and martyrdom is a thing of the past. That's my mission - to help you find your way back to yourself and your happiness. You will fuel your life and the lives of all those around you.

You are here to live, live, live!!! What is the f*cking point otherwise?! It is not to get up, go to work, look after kids, pay bills, do the washing and then die. Yes, those things are necessary evils, but why not make it all work for you and round you so that you thrive through life, not merely survive. I'm not saying let's all go party like it's 1999 and f*ck the side effects. I'm saying that life is meant to be fun, a pleasure and enjoyed when you know where you are going, then every day feels like a celebration. When you are truly happy, the side effect is wellbeing; there is no denying it.

I have witnessed too many people choosing stress over happiness. They are losing their whole lives trying to keep things together on a hamster wheel that only stops when you step off. Striving for more, more, more to keep up with the boring Jones'. It's not worth it. It's not life. That's somebody else's shallow life. The Jones's are dull.

You do you because the best person to play the part of you is you. You cannot be anyone else than who you are because you don't fit the job spec. You know who you are. You have just forgotten.

I am here to get you to step the f*ck away from the hamster wheel of overwhelm, the shoulds and the Jones's. Then catapult you into the technicolour glory that is the life you came to this earth to live. It's time to write a new story and create a new narrative that flows through you with ease and grace. It's time to embody your true self, and I am here to hold your hand and cheerlead you until you are ready to fly.

You are your salvation, and you and only you have the power to style your best life. As your empathetic guide and entertaining sidekick, I'm here, but I take no prisoners! I am here to hold YOU entirely accountable to yourself because that is the crux of life.

YOU.

You are the beginning, the middle and the end. You are the greatest creation. You are here to live a life of your design. You know what that life looks like because it calls to you on the breeze and tugs at your heart, and if it isn't already, it will start slapping you around the face and kicking you up the arse. It will continue until you acknowledge it and face your mother f*cking self.

I know. That's what got me here. I am following my calling. I took a massive risk on myself to permit you to do the same (and I'm very happy for you to blame it all on me!)

22

Permission to be f*cking happy

If you take nothing else from this book other than the premise that there is no better tonic for your health than a well-lived life. Whatever that means to you. Then I have won.

We are only working towards death. The journey is here and now, and I can throw cliché after cliché at you. But, after major trial and error, I can officially declare that there is nothing to fear but fear itself.

Faith in myself is my religion - the spiritual healers didn't resonate with me until I permitted myself to be f*cking happy.

When we live in complete alignment with ourselves, we can create miracles. And, we allow ourselves to be happy, and that happiness puts pay to the dis-ease in our bodies that is borne out of stress and worry.

I have grown up with privilege, yes but perspective.

We are like goldfish. We grow to the size of our bowl/surroundings. There's no point in me becoming poor to help the poor or starving to help the starving. The best way we can serve others is to strive for better. To see the pain caused by not helping one another and do something about it.

Stop trying so hard. When we try too hard, we become stressed. An aligned life deals only in flow. When we are in flow, life is easy. The waves lap in and out, the sun shines, and our energy circuit flows round and round and round. The circuit breakers and dysfunction are things of the past. We get to slow down, enjoy the journey and smell the roses.

Understand that your intuition is your internal guidance system, and your desires are there to motivate you to make you grow! If you didn't have any desires, you wouldn't bother to do anything because what would be the point? Yes, your desires may seem utterly frivolous, but who cares? There would be no beauty in the human world if no one had frivolous desires. We can't all be f*cking saints!

There would be very little growth; without the rule-breakers, trouble makers, and non-conformists. I'm not talking about felons; I'm talking about those who won't be boxed in by society's rules. The most successful entrepreneurs and artists went their own way. They pushed against the system and did what their hearts told them to do, not their heads.

Speaking of desires, you need to welcome envy and jealousy into your world, but just treat them as a signal that you also want something someone else has. Instead of being bitchy about it, wish them well and start working towards it. I can't remember who wrote this mantra, but it has always helped me. When someone has what I would like, I say to myself, "good for you and for me too". See it as a sign that it is achievable because anything is possible when you put your mind to it. Desires aren't planted without you having the capability to achieve them.

You need to accept that the only way to a healthy and fulfilling life is to embrace who you are, follow your intuition and work towards achieving your desires. They are your roadmap. Not what society tells you is the roadmap. That one is a safety card; it isn't advice for living a fulfilled life.

The human spirit is insane. It is like the wind or the tides. It can't be seen, but it can be felt, and the power behind it is immense. Without it, we would be limp and lifeless. Trying to contain it is like herding cats. It is to be embraced and revered. It is what makes you, you. It is your 'self'. It is a God that is channelling through you. It is a force of nature to be reckoned with, and there is no stopping it because if you try to contain it, you'll make yourself ill!

My biggest driver since my divorce has been my children. I am responsible for setting an example of how to live well for my two little girls. They learn everything from the overt and not-so overt inputs around them. I am a major source, and that is a big responsibility. I want them to trailblaze through life. I want them to believe so strongly in themselves that nothing and no one can hurt them. I want them to be titanium. The best way to teach them this is by embodying that ethos through everything I do and embracing the f*cking wild spirit that courses through me and you.

It has been said that the brave do not live forever, but the cautious do not live at all.

Please take this as permission to be f*cking happy.

Acknowledgments

Mum and Roger, thank you for modelling a lifestyle (so many holidays!), strength of character & values system that I aspire to and for giving me the opportunity to save myself. I'm sure it's not been easy for you to watch me go through this period in my life but your faith has been a guiding light for me to find faith in myself and for that I will be forever grateful.

Dad what can I say, your spirit, humour & sense of adventure are the character traits that I revel in but learning to balance them with responsibility has been my journey! Thank you for letting me find solace in the sunshine with you and enjoying rosé, gambas pil pil & endless walks, silly jokes and racket sports!

My sisters, you have been my main stays. Keeping me safe when I wasn't able to anymore. Picking me up off the ground when I felt like I couldn't go on. Reminding me that I am loved.

My friends old and new (and some solely online) that checked in on me, that went out of their way to make sure that I didn't feel alone and to wrap their arms around me when I cried (which has been a lot). I will forever be grateful for having you in my life. For providing me with some of your strength when I was all out. For reminding me of what life is about when I didn't know anymore.

All the men who rejected me and made me feel like I wasn't good enough. Thank you for teaching me how to love myself fully and for the entertainment along the way!

Sam Houghton your guidance on this book is the only reason that it is actually a thing. Without your encouragement and unwavering faith in me it would never have come to fruition. Thank you for being so very very you in order to allow me to be so very, very me.

Holly, Carly, Luma, Riikka, Annalie & all of you who gifted me your services in order to help me get myself off of the ground. I can honestly say that without your kindness I don't know where I would be. Not only did you nourish me with your gifts but you restored my faith in humanity.

Alicia thank you for calmly listening to me for all these years on our walks and runs and supporting me on this journey to happiness. Your friendship is a gift.

Claire & Neal your orange dinners (and espresso martinis) have saved me and brought so much joy to our lives. Your warm welcome has never gone unnoticed.

Ellie & Emma my best witchy friends, you have reminded me that it is possible to live well and have fun at the same time. You offer me so much inspiration and so much support all washed down with bubbles. What more could a girl ask for.

Rich you demonstrated a lifestyle to me that helped me realise what I truly valued in my life and I thank you for that, none of what happened was in vain it was simply part of our journey.

Contact

If you would like to find out more or to contact the author head to:

www.theconsciouslifestylist.co.uk

IG @theconsciouslifestylist/@styleyourbestlife

hello@sarah-miller.co.uk

Printed in Great Britain
by Amazon

40381118R00131